Fully Human in Christ

"Todd Speidell's book, *Fully Human in Christ*, is a wise and winsome account of how Thomas F. Torrance's Trinitarian and Christocentric theology is inextricably connected to a profound Christian ethic, including a social ethic as well. His work is a cathartic antidote to the many criticisms that Torrance's theology lacks a robust ethical dimension. Speidell's clever subtitle, *The Incarnation as the End of Ethics*, encapsulates his central thesis that Christ's vicarious humanity ends all ours attempts to 'do good or be good' apart from who Christ is and what Christ has done on our behalf and in our place. In place of every autonomous ethic is a radically new and different gracious ethical participation in Christ's vicarious humanity. This participation does in no way negate or replace our humanity, but rather frees, personalizes, humanizes, and reconciles us in all our relations with God and others, overcoming all bigotry, hatred, and every other barrier we create and maintain to secure and justify ourselves and people like us in alienation from God and others. Having grown up amidst the violence, injustice, and urban unrest in Paterson, NJ, during the 1960s and '70s, Speidell's penetrating, sustained, and captivating thinking of ethics in dialogue with Torrance is a profound, joyous, and hopeful account of what a Christian ethic really is. Scholars, pastors, students, and others interested in Christian theology and ethics will be challenged and encouraged by Speidell's contributions in this book."

—**ELMER M. COLYER**
Professor of Systematic Theology, Stanley Professor of Wesley Studies,
University of Dubuque Theological Seminary

"Todd Speidell has written a wonderful book, not simply about T. F. Torrance's overlooked contributions to thinking theologically about ethics, but more broadly about the reality of reconciliation and the triune God's unwavering commitment to redeem creation. Speaking with great insight and candor, Speidell sets the record on Torrance straight, helping us to see that Christ is the end of ethics, thereby abolishing our attempts at self-justification and autonomous ethics in favor of His vicarious humanity in our place and on our behalf. Students and teachers of Christian doctrine and ethics are very well-served by this clear, judicious, and compelling account and appropriation of one of the most important English-speaking theologians of the twentieth century."

—**CHRISTOPHER R. J. HOLMES**
Senior Lecturer in Theology, University of Otago

"Relying on the thinking of Karl Barth, Thomas F. Torrance, James B. Torrance, Dietrich Bonhoeffer, Ray S. Anderson, and others, Todd Speidell thoughtfully and skillfully challenges readers to focus on who Jesus was and is as the incarnate revealer and reconciler to understand the true meaning of Christian ethics and liberation in a way that upholds rather than negates a properly functioning social ethic. Along the way he offers helpful analysis and critique of various views that tend toward a Pelagian vision of grace or some version of conditional salvation and thus obscure what it means to participate in Christ's vicarious humanity and therefore in the new creation. His discussion of Torrance's theological ethics offers a particularly convincing and compelling defense of Torrance against allegations that his emphasis on Christ supplants rather than establishes true human freedom and action. This is a book that is refreshingly Christological, Trinitarian, and soteriological in the best sense. Readers will find here a serious and informative discussion of exactly how dogmatics informs ethics when the living Christ, rather than dogmatics, is, and remains, the criterion."

—**PAUL D. MOLNAR**
Professor of Systematic Theology, St. John's University, Queens, NY

Fully Human in Christ

The Incarnation as the End of Christian Ethics

Todd Speidell

WIPF & STOCK · Eugene, Oregon

Fully Human in Christ
The Incarnation as the End of Christian Ethics

Copyright © 2016 Todd Speidell. All rights reserved. Except for brief quotations in critical publications or reviews, no part of this book may be reproduced in any manner without prior written permission from the publisher. Write: Permissions, Wipf and Stock Publishers, 199 W. 8th Ave., Suite 3, Eugene, OR 97401.

Wipf & Stock
An Imprint of Wipf and Stock Publishers
199 W. 8th Ave., Suite 3
Eugene, OR 97401

www.wipfandstock.com

paperback isbn: 978-1-4982-9637-3
hardcover isbn: 978-1-4982-9369-7
ebook isbn: 978-1-4982-9638-0

Manufactured in the U.S.A.   October 18, 2016 10:27 AM

Table of Contents

A Personal Introduction, Chapter Summaries, and Personal Acknowledgments — vii

1. The Soteriological Suspension of Ethics in the Theology of T. F. Torrance — 1

2. Incarnational Social Ethics — 38

3. A Christological Critique of Adjectival Theologies — 67

4. A Trinitarian Ontology of Persons in Society — 87

5. The Humanity of God and the Healing of Humanity — 105

6. Theological Anthropology as a Basis for Christian Ethics in the Theology of Ray S. Anderson — 119

Appendix A: A Radio Interview with Todd Speidell on Evangelical Social Ethics — 133

Appendix B: God, Woody Allen, and Job — 141

To Chris Kettler,
with gratitude for theological conversation
and even more so for friendship

A Personal Introduction

My interest in "theological ethics" began before I knew it as an academic discipline. As a child and teenager in the 1960s and '70s, I encountered the urban unrest of the time in Paterson, New Jersey. Racial violence occurred daily, whether on the streets or in the schools, and de facto segregation largely governed neighborhood residences and interpersonal friendships. While civil rights protests and legislation were underway, basic issues of safety and human matters of justice were very much in jeopardy.

My parents, Rev. Henry Speidell and Mrs. Ruth Speidell, devoted their lives to urban ministry as they raised their four children in Paterson, which was a paradigm of the violent restlessness of the times. They were conservative Christians and Republicans, and yet their hearts went out to the poor, distressed, and neglected residents of inner city America. While Dad was working on a Ph.D. degree in Old Testament and Semitic Languages in inner city Chicago, he felt called to urban ministry because he thought the church's presence in American cities was too often absent. Two of my three siblings, David and Karen, did not survive due in part to the effects of our upbringing. Ch. 6 of this book tells Karen's story.

The movies *Lean on Me* (1989) and *The Hurricane* (1999) depict the chaos, racism, and tumult of my hometown, Paterson, NJ, in the '60s and '70s. In the first film, Morgan Freeman plays the role of Joe Clark, Principal of Paterson's East Side High School, our rival high school as students of John F. Kennedy High School. Joe Clark had made the cover of *Time Magazine* in 1988 for his unorthodox methods of discipline, including carrying a baseball bat to restore and maintain order in the violent classrooms, bathrooms, and hallways of East Side.

In the second film, Denzel Washington stars as Rubin "Hurricane" Carter, a victim of the racist Paterson Police Dept. and subject of the 1976 Bob Dylan song of the same name. Whatever the level of accuracy of this film, it depicts the Paterson Police Dept. that I knew in Paterson, even though I was white and Rubin Carter was black. As I watch this movie, it is ironic to see the moment when a young Rubin becomes the target of an unsavoury white man, because it occurs in the very place where I was mugged by black youths. The scene was filmed at Paterson's Great Falls of

A Personal Introduction

the Passaic River, which Alexander Hamilton picked to plan Paterson as the first industrial city of the United States.

A literary reference to my hometown is William Carlos Williams' classic and lengthy poem, *Paterson*, which follows the course of the Passaic River and Passaic Falls (later named the Great Falls when Gerald Ford visited to honor this historic site and declare it a national landmark during a 1976 presidential campaign stop, which I witnessed in my late teenage years). Just as Williams features the Falls in his epic poem, the crashing sounds of the mighty water upon the rocks remind me both of the beauty and of the destructiveness of the natural and human order of things.

My older brother, David, and I were playing by the Falls one winter day when the surrounding grounds were snowy and icy. David slipped and started sliding down a steep and slick slope toward the unforgiving Falls. Based on pure instinct and with no time for thought, I grabbed David with one hand and a fence with the other, averting a disastrous and untimely death for David. While Paterson and its Falls had redemptive meaning for William Carlos Williams, it served for me as an initial and prereflective stimulus to consider God and his reconciling work in our turbulent world. God redeems his created order, including Christ's full restoration of our humanity to its proper place in relationship to God our Creator and Father. When Christ assumed our humanity, he healed and redeemed it.

As I write many years later, this book is about being fully human and not dehumanized by our fellow human beings or the principalities and powers of this world. Christ took upon himself our sinful and alienated humanity, redeeming and restoring us as children of God and as brothers and sisters in him. He has said No to all of our attempts to undo his reconciliation of all things unto God. He is not captive to political slogans that divide instead of unite, such as two current polarized movements: Black Lives Matter vs. All Lives Matter. While such dichotomies captivate the American media and public alike, Christ as Reconciler breaks down these dividing walls of hostility. The Jewish man Jesus takes on our humanity — in all of its racial, ethnic, historical, economic, and geographical diversity — and both judges and heals it. He says No to our ongoing attempt to erect and perpetuate barriers of anger, hatred, and bigotry, and he says Yes to his Father's mission to reconcile all things, all peoples, all cultures *in him*. *Christ's humanity matters*, and our lives matter more, not less, as we receive our true humanity in him by the gift of his Spirit.

A Personal Introduction

The perspective of this book is that *Christ* is the ground of Christian ethics. Firstly, he is the terminating end of *"ethics"* — understood as the *autonomous* attempt to do good or be good apart from God in Christ. He abolishes our self-justifying and self-defeating efforts based on moral or religious law in favor of justification by God's grace alone. He reverses the Fall, where the original human couple opted for an ethic of individual autonomy and abstract morality (the good, the true, the beautiful of Gen. 3:6) in place of God's concrete command and gracious freedom for humanity.

Secondly, the incarnate Christ is the *end* of ethics in a double sense: He not only disables and discontinues our human attempts to justify ourselves before God and others, but he also fulfills what he destroys because he is the new and true man on behalf of the redemption of all people. Christ negates our futile attempts to be free and independent apart from God *and* he overcomes the split between God and humanity we effected in our sinful and rebellious humanity. When God assumed our disordered human nature in Christ, he healed us from within the depths of our being. He now permits and commands us to be who we are and are becoming in him.

An ethic of grace in Christ speaks of a new reality that goes beyond the rationalizing emphases and tendencies of standard ethical theories. The incarnation of God in Christ, the vicarious humanity of Christ in our place and on our behalf, locates the reality of human reconciliation in God's own being-as-love and unrelenting resolve to redeem his fallen creation. A *Christian* ethic, then, calls us to follow *Christ* and participate in him as he continues by his Spirit God's good work on behalf of the world. This book's contribution to the field of Christian ethics grounds ethics in God's justifying and redemptive grace. As such, it witnesses to the reconciling person and work of Jesus Christ *for us*.

It is unfortunate and tragic that many Christian theologians give way to political parties and platforms, passing winds and fads of our day, in lieu of attesting to what God has done and how he continues to redeem humanity as his children, as fellow brothers and sisters in Christ. If this book has any value, it is this: It dispels theology made in our own image on behalf of this cause or another and instead considers what the Word of God is doing in our world, which suggests a filial rather than a political ethic. Christ breaks down our dichotomies and unites all people in his humanity, whether we be male or female, black or white, Asian or Latino, rich or poor, Republican or Democrat, or other walls of division throughout the world.

A Personal Introduction

Christ is the end of ethics since he sets aside all of our autonomous and self-justifying projects and frees us to participate in what he does on our behalf as we live in union with him in all that it means to be fully human.

Chapter Summaries

Earlier versions of these chapters and appendices appeared as published essays, which now appear in revised form with an acknowledgement to the original publishers. While these book chapters do have overlapping material due to their original form as independent essays, each may still be read profitably on its own. Nonetheless, I have revised these essays to achieve consistency between chapters and provide coherence as a book on behalf of articulating a trinitarian-incarnational social ethic.

The first chapter, "The Soteriological Suspension of Ethics in the Theology of T. F. Torrance" (recently published in *Participatio: The Journal of the Thomas F. Torrance Theological Fellowship*), is the foundational essay of this book — not despite his supposed neglect of ethics, as some critics mistakenly charge, but precisely because of his *intentional* and *soteriological* suspension of autonomous ethics as a human attempt to justify themselves through moral law, effort, and virtue. His critics miss that he implicitly included a trinitarian-incarnational ethic of grace throughout his entire theological and scientific work. He also explicitly articulated a Christian ethic based on Christ's vicarious humanity: his atoning work in our place and on our behalf throughout his life, death, and resurrection. Finally, he did occasionally address concrete moral issues, and I will include as evidence his views on women in ministry, God-language, abortion, telling and doing the truth, and juridical law in light of modern physical law. His critics have failed to perceive his theological ethic as integral to his entire work, which proclaims the personalizing and humanizing mediation of Christ in all realms of life — including not only the private or personal dimension of human life but also the social, historical, and political structures of human society and even of the cosmos itself. Torrance's critics themselves, in short, have neglected the central role in Torrance's theology of a Christian ethic rooted in God's grace, which encompasses, sustains, and transforms the entire human and created order. As he often said with a favorite phrase of his, it is "precisely the opposite" of the critics' claims. This first chapter lays a foundation for the rest of the book, which mines the rich theology of TF Torrance's ethic of reconciliation. Of the growing secondary literature about Torrance, none has appreciated his distinctly theological contribution to the field of social ethics.

The third and fourth chapters, "A Christological Critique of Adjectival Theologies" and "A Trinitarian Ontology of Persons in Society," appeared in earlier form in the *Scottish Journal of Theology*, with the latter essay serving as a sequel to the former. My christological critique of liberationist, feminist, postcolonial, and other adjectival theologies of our day — and I make no pretense to being a comprehensive or contemporary catalogue of such multifarious and anthropocentric theologies — is admittedly a way of constructing an alternative way of doing theology in dialogue with various representatives of politicized theologies. I constructively develop a trinitarian-incarnational social ethic based on who God is for us, not on whom we want God to be, for what I call the "ecopersonal" dimensions of society.

The second and fifth chapters, "Incarnational Social Ethics" and "The Humanity of God and the Healing of Humanity," were published in the two *Festschriften* for Ray S. Anderson. Like his mentor TF Torrance, Ray is not considered a "social ethicist," but his theological anthropology based on the theology of Barth, Bonhoeffer, and Torrance profoundly addresses issues of human and social life. I constructively developed his theology in a previously published essay in *Cultural Encounters*, which forms the sixth chapter, "Theological Anthropology as Basis for Ethics in the Theology of Ray S. Anderson." It theologically discusses alcoholism and its effects upon ordinary people in need of something other than drink, which took my sister's life. As Ray the pastor preferred, I've used the case study approach based on the actual experience of people in need.

I have included two appendices, which also were previously published. The first was a radio interview that later appeared in *Participatio: The Journal of the Thomas F. Torrance Theological Fellowship* as a transcript from a Christian radio station in Ohio that interviewed me about a distinctively Christian and evangelical approach to social ethics. It could be helpful as a concise and less formal overview of the theological-ethical concerns of this book. The second appendix, "God, Woody Allen, and Job," appeared in *Christian Scholar's Review* and articulated a theology of the vicarious humanity of Christ in dialogue with the skeptical, agnostic, Woody Allen, whose modernist anti-theology pales in depth compared to the ancient biblical poet Job. I include it as an example of relating my theological concerns to culture and the implicit worldviews prevalent in film. It is also a testament to my love for the book of Job.

Personal Acknowledgements

My professors and mentors, Ray Anderson, Geoffrey Bromiley, J. B. Torrance, and T. F. Torrance, have influenced me and my publications well beyond their lives. While only JB might qualify to some extent as a theologian of "social ethics," all four were primarily ministers and theologians of the Gospel. I am grateful to have had these pastoral and incarnational theologians as early influences on my theological mind and personal ministry in my various vocational settings.

My good friend Paul Molnar has become an informal mentor. Over many years now he has faithfully and graciously replied, often in great detail, to my countless emails with questions about T. F. Torrance's theology, usually accompanied with discussion of baseball (Paul being a NY Mets' fan and I a NY Yankees' fan). While I acknowledge him in a footnote in my foundational chapter on T. F. Torrance and ethics, I add him here as an important friend and trusted adviser. His influence on my theological mind extends well beyond what I could express in one footnote.

El Colyer has become a trusted friend and confidant. Our discussions are usually more personal than theological; his friendship, counsel, and wisdom have sustained me when I needed support. He always provides positive words about my publication projects. Such encouraging words of kindness are good to hear when one invests the time required for peer-reviewed publications. I thank him for reading and commenting on this book.

My dear friend Chris Kettler, to whom this book is dedicated, encouraged me to take courses with Ray Anderson and T. F. Torrance, especially while I was misguidedly trying to find my way as a young seminarian. Contemporary theological models and issues preoccupied my mind, but Chris challenged me to think more seriously and *theologically* about theology, which is to say about God and his agenda for his created world. As God said to Job, "Where were you . . . ?" My theological training (in chronological order) with Ray Anderson, T. F. Torrance, Geoffrey Bromiley, and J. B. Torrance initiated for me a conversion of my mind, which caused me to look for new spectacles to see afresh what God says and does to set aright his fallen and fractured world. I am indebted to Chris for

Personal Acknowledgements

introducing me to my mentors and encouraging me to write and publish this book.

I am grateful to Jim Tedrick, Managing Editor of Wipf and Stock Publishers, for his support of Torrance scholarship in general and my publications in particular. A word of thanks also goes to three staff members of *Participatio: The Journal of the Thomas F. Torrance Theological Fellowship*. Asst. Editor Jonathan Kleis and Copy Editor Steve Chaffee carefully unearthed errors and helpfully suggested clarifications. Jock Stein, Production Editor, formatted and prepared this book for publication. I of course am responsible for any lingering imperfections.

Chapter 1

The Soteriological Suspension of Ethics in the Theology of T. F. Torrance

Introduction: Critique of Torrance's "neglect of ethics"

T. F. Torrance's theology reflected his broad concerns as a churchman, professor, author, editor, and minister of the Gospel.[1] John Webster et al., however, have levelled the charge that he neglected ethics. I will argue that this criticism is wrong for three reasons:

1. Torrance intentionally suspended, not neglected, "ethics" — especially as an autonomous field of study and a human attempt at self-justification through morality, and yet one can read his entire theology as an ethic of reconciliation.

2. He clearly articulated a Christian ethic as theologically grounded in the incarnation and atonement and understood it as a reconciliation of all things in Christ (not only human relationships with God but also with others and even of the very space-time structures of the polis and the cosmos).

3. He specifically addressed concrete matters of personal, social, and political responsibility, such as women in ministry, abortion, God-language, truth-telling, and law — and whether or not one agrees with his conclusions, he concerned himself with these issues as human and theological concerns.

David Fergusson's essay, "The Ascension of Christ,"[2] criticizes "the relative absence of the ethical and political significance of the ascension, not

---

[1] For a brief introduction, see my "What Scientists Get, and Theologians Don't, About Thomas F. Torrance" in *First Things* 6.26.13. Also see John Webster's excellent biographical essay on Torrance in *Biographical Memoirs of Fellows of the British Academy*, XIII, 2014, 417-36.

[2] "The Ascension of Christ: Its Significance in the Theology of T. F. Torrance" (a lecture delivered to the T. F. Torrance Theological Fellowship at the American Academy of Religion in Atlanta, November, 2010, and published in *Participatio: The Journal of the*

least given its greater prominence in Barth. For Torrance, the divine-human relation tends to be largely a private one," with only occasional hints of a "wider sociopolitical significance . . . Yet the important relations and movements in Torrance are, as it were, vertical rather than horizontal . . . His occasional excursions into Christian ethics tend to be confined to areas of private rather than social morality — for example, marriage and abortion. There is little about social justice, human equality, or the peaceable kingdom. The focus is generally doxological rather than ethical, whereas the royal Psalms and Jesus' teaching of the kingdom point to ways in which these can be integrated."[3]

During the original presentation of his paper, Fergusson cited John Webster's criticism that Torrance "neglected ethics." As Webster himself criticizes Torrance, the doctrine of the vicarious humanity of Christ evacuates humans of their own humanity: "To talk of justification is to talk of the way in which our being lies beyond us in the true man Jesus."[4] Webster levels two criticisms of the vicarious humanity of Christ, which is a cardinal doctrine in Torrance's theology and will be the basis of my reply to his critique: "The first concerns the adequacy of an account of justification which does not underline the primacy of the moral. . . . A second question concerns the conception of the vicarious humanity of Christ . . . Stated very simply, the vigorous affirmation of *solus Christus* may well threaten rather than validate man." He concludes: "The question poses itself: does Christ's fraternity with the human race validate or invalidate our humanity?"[5] We will revisit these themes throughout this essay: "the primacy of the moral" (in which case of course T. F. Torrance did "neglect ethics"!); and whether the vicarious humanity of Christ "may well threaten rather than validate man" or his "fraternity" with and for us might somehow "invalidate our humanity" (which is precisely the opposite of Torrance's clear and explicit view of the vicarious humanity of Christ on behalf of our humanity).

Thomas F. Torrance Theological Fellowship, Vol. 3 (2012): 92-107. All of Vol. 3 is devoted to Torrance's emphasis on the *interrelationship* of incarnation and atonement. Also see Vol. 5 (2015) on the vicarious humanity of Christ and ethics, in which this book chapter originally appeared in essay form (56-90). Also see in the same volume Christopher Holmes' excellent essay, "'Renewal Through Union': Thomas F. Torrance on the New Basis of Ethics" (45-55).

3 Ibid., 106.

4 *Eberhard Jüngel: An Introduction to his Theology* (Cambridge: CUP, 1986), 102, and see n. 49, which extends his critique of Jüngel to Torrance.

5 Ibid., 102-3.

The Soteriological Suspension of Ethics

Webster's early criticism of Torrance's view of the vicarious humanity of Christ appears in two essays on the concept of the imitation of Christ.[6] Webster asks: "If Christians are what they are by virtue of their participation in the benefits of God's saving acts in Christ, then what room is left for human ethical activity in our account of what makes a person into the person he or she is?" (Webster here blurs the issue of our identity in Christ before God with our psycho-social identity that we forge for ourselves though personal agency and moral action.) The New Testament imitation motif "may help us hold together the derivative character of human morality and its character as a human project involving choice, conscious allegiance and deliberation."[7] He charges certain Protestant theological ethics (of which Torrance is a prime example) with the claim that "the subject as agent with duration through history all but vanishes, displaced by the sole agency of Christ." (Here he fails to grasp that the vicarious humanity of Christ renders our own faithfulness and obedience both possible and necessary: we *may* and we *must*, both *in union with him*.) "The core of the debate," he rightly summarizes, "is thus whether we allow any intrinsic connexion between Christological-soteriological affirmations and affirmations about human morality."[8]

Webster notes the Protestant anxiety and criticism that an emphasis on *imitatio Christi* fails to "root ethics in soteriology," but he counters that "Christ's action is more than vicarious: it is evocative, it constitutes a summons to a properly derivative mimesis." He cites Karl Barth's view that the actions of persons in Christ "'correspond' to Jesus Christ's own acts . . . [B]ecause of their gracious participation in God through Christ, Christians are enabled to act in such a way that their acts correspond to the acts of the Saviour."[9] Such action is derivative but nonetheless analogous, enabling "policy-formation for those whose lives are bound up with that of Jesus Christ" and explicating the "*kinds* of divine activity" in concrete circumstances that humans should imitate through "individual choice, obedience, and action."[10]

In these two early essays, Webster begins his criticism that Barth's theology deals more adequately with ethics than does Torrance's. In a

---

6 "The Imitation of Christ" in *Tyndale Bulletin* 37 (1986) 95-120 and "Christology, Imitability and Ethics" in *Scottish Journal of Theology* 39:3 (1986) 309-326.

7 "The Imitation of Christ," 95-6.

8 Ibid., 105, 107.

9 "Christology, Imitability and Ethics," 313, 321, 323.

10 Ibid., 324-6.

later essay,¹¹ he makes explicit the contrast between Barth's and Torrance's treatment of human agency by noting Torrance's critique of Barth's view of believer's baptism, which Torrance considers "deeply inconsistent" with "the vicarious character of Jesus' obedience in his own baptism." Torrance views "the acts of Jesus as solely vicarious," Webster avers, whereas "Barth sees them as representative acts which are nevertheless more than simply completed events containing proleptically our involvement: they are 'really an imperative' (*CD* IV/4:67)." Webster concludes that Barth's view of grace "does not furnish us with excuses for inaction . . . a kind of dependence where our actions make no significant contribution to the fabric of our lives."¹²

Webster then establishes a substantial treatment of Barth's moral theology in two monumental books.¹³ In *Barth's Ethics of Reconciliation*, he summarizes the contrast he sees between Barth and Torrance on human agency and ethics:

> Though at many points Barth will say similar things, his real divergence from Torrance concerns the covenantal character of the relation between God and humanity, which Barth sees as ethically fundamental (in that it affirms the inalienable difference-in-relation of God and humanity), but which is obscured in Torrance's exclusive stress upon the vicarious character of Jesus' being and act in relation to humanity. In Torrance's account of the matter, Jesus' humanity threatens to absorb that of others; in Barth's account,

---

11 "The Christian in Revolt. Some Reflections on The Christ Life," in *Reckoning with Barth: Essays in Commemoration of the Centenary of Karl Barth's Birth*, ed. Nigel Biggar (London: Mowbray, 1988) 119-44.

12 Ibid., 126.

13 *Barth's Ethics of Reconciliation* (Cambridge: CUP, 1995) and *Barth's Moral Theology: Human Action in Barth's Thought* (Grand Rapids: Eerdmans, 1998). Even Alister McGrath, brilliant biographer of *T. F. Torrance: An Intellectual Biography* (Edinburgh: T&T Clark, 1999), cites these two works by Webster as self-evident proof that "Barth addressed some issues on which Torrance has not chosen to focus in depth, such as the foundations and structures of Christian ethics" (112. n. 1). While Barth did develop more specialized discussion of ethics in relation to dogmatics, this essay will prove that the whole of Torrance's theology concerns itself with this exact foundational and structural issue: Christian ethics are grounded in Christ's reconciling work, not in our own human morality, which means that we may obey God from the heart with gratitude throughout our entire lives. Torrance's evangelical ethic is deeply grounded in God's grace in fundamental agreement with Barth, contrary to Webster's overstated contrast between Torrance and Barth.

The Soteriological Suspension of Ethics

Jesus' humanity graciously evokes corresponding patterns of being and doing on the part of those whom it constitutes.[14]

Paul Molnar better captures, however, the basic similarity and essential agreement of Barth's and Torrance's Christian ethic without posing these odd dichotomies embedded in Webster's reading:

> For Barth and Torrance there is only one possible choice that is enabled and required by the risen Lord himself, and that is to choose him and thus to exercise free obedience . . . The essence of faith then is to accept as right what God has done for us and in us. This takes place in and through the Holy Spirit acting for us and in us. While Torrance does not develop his thought on this subject explicitly with respect to Christian ethics in any sense as thoroughly as Barth has, he nonetheless would agree that true human knowledge and action are possible because they find their meaning outside themselves and only in Christ.[15]

One should note that, unlike Karl Barth in Basel, T. F. Torrance in Edinburgh taught theology and not ethics, the latter being relegated to New College's Dept. of Christian Ethics and Practical Theology — a dualism that no doubt bothered Torrance more so than his critics![16] Nonetheless, Torrance does share with Barth a thoroughly integrated theological ethic (contra Webster), which relativizes autonomous ethics by the vicarious humanity of the incarnate, crucified, and risen Christ. How Webster's assertion, "Christ's action is more than vicarious," criticizes Torrance's theological ethic is not entirely clear, given that for Torrance *Christ's vicarious humanity, his faith(fulness) and obedience, both permits and thus obligates us to be who we are and are becoming in him.*

Torrance's understanding of God's grace, contra-Webster, commits us unequivocally to action. At the same time, we acknowledge that Christ's

---

14 Ibid., 171.

15 Paul D. Molnar, *Incarnation & Resurrection: Toward a Contemporary Understanding* (Grand Rapids: Eerdmans, 2007), 150. Also see his excellent book *Thomas F. Torrance: Theologian of the Trinity* (Burlington, VT: Ashgate, 2009). Dr. Molnar, Prof. of Systematic Theology at St. John's University, New York, gave generously of his time to help clarify and confirm my thesis that Torrance articulated a clear Christian ethic based on the vicarious humanity of Christ.

16 Alasdair Heron made this point to me as a practical, albeit secondary, explanation for why Barth's explicit treatment of ethics (e.g. *Church Dogmatics* III/4) exceeded Torrance's. David Fergusson, Prof. of Divinity in New College Edinburgh, confirmed Heron's claim and also provided gracious and helpful comments on my essay.

vicarious humanity means he has already rendered human covenant-obedience to the Father in our place and on our behalf. As we cling to Christ, we participate in him and his work as we live in union with him; we all the more, not less, act as God's children. God's grace toward us never renders our participatory obedience superfluous, as is clear throughout Torrance's entire theology and life.

Webster does cite and quote from what he correctly calls "a magisterial essay" by Torrance (in Webster's discussion of canon, but he misses that this passage directly and explicitly relates to Torrance's ethic too!):

> Jesus Christ is God's self-address to man, but this self-address in order to achieve its end had to penetrate, take form and domicile itself within the address of man to man, as the Word of Christ abiding among men. *The reciprocity established between God and man in Jesus Christ had to create room for itself within the reciprocities of human society, and the Word of God which had come 'plumb down from above' had to deploy itself in the horizontal dimensions of human existence in order to continue its speaking and acting throughout history.* This involved the formation of a nucleus within the speaker-hearer relations of men, corresponding to and grounded in the communion between God and man embodied in Jesus Christ, as the controlling basis among believers for the extended communication of the Word of God, and the translation of the self-witness of Christ into witness to Christ, answering the normative pattern of His obedient humanity, as the specific form for the proclamation of God's Word to all men.[17]

This essay by Torrance, "The Word of God and the Response of Man," will begin my introductory response to the curious critique of Webster. Jesus Christ, for Torrance, is both God's Word to humanity *and* the perfect human response to God because Jesus is both one with God and one with us. Because Jesus acts as one among us and for us, we actually do share in his vicarious humanity as we participate and live in union with him by the presence and power of his Spirit. Rejecting Fergusson's charge that Torrance's theology accents what is "vertical rather than horizontal," what is "private rather than social," I will argue that these antinomies are instead integrated and integral throughout his entire work, through

---

17 *Word and Church: Essays in Christian Dogmatics* (Edinburgh: T&T Clark, 2001), 33-4; n. 54 cites Torrance's "The Word of God and the Response of Man" in *God and Rationality* (Oxford: OUP, 1971), 151f. Emphasis added to underscore key counter-evidence to the Webster-Fergusson thesis.

a Christian ethic based on the atonement, and by specific discussions of women in ministry, God-language, abortion, law, and "doing the truth" and "telling the truth." Irrespective of whether one agrees with his conclusions, his view of the vicarious humanity of Christ does not "invalidate our humanity" or provide "excuses for inaction." I will argue that Webster's summary critique of Torrance — "The core of the debate is thus whether we allow any intrinsic connexion between Christological-soteriological affirmations and affirmations about human morality" — fails to understand Torrance's unitary theological ethic.[18] The remainder of this chapter will offer a rejoinder to the critique by presenting a positive case for Torrance's trinitarian-incarnational ethic of grace, which pervades the whole of his theology and is as radical, thorough-going, and inclusive as our reconciliation in Christ.

---

18 R. Michael Allen badly overstates the Webster critique in *The Christ's Faith: A Dogmatic Account* (London: T&T Clark, 209). I will note a few examples (with italics added to highlight his overstatements): Torrance has "so emphasized the work of Christ for us, vicariously, that the place of Christ's faith as *any* sort of ethical norm seems *displaced*" (19), including "the *opposition* Torrance places between Christ's activity and that of Christians" as a "*unilateral* emphasis" (19, n. 58). He ends up *"denying any* discernable (sic) moral space for Christian ethical action" (197). Allen cites Webster's argument that "Torrance flattens the relation of Christ and Christian to vicarious representation and *nothing else*" (197), but in the process he himself compresses and flattens Webster's critique. He complains of Torrance's "*vacuous* moral ontology" and "his denial of *any* imitative function of the Christ's faith" (198), which is another overstatement with no textual support from Torrance himself. He concludes with a final instance of his bald critique of Torrance: "soteriology cannot be *simply* conflated with Christology" (213). The more recent book by Nathan Hieb, *Christ Crucified in a Suffering World: The Unity of Atonement and Liberation* (Minneapolis: Fortress, 2013), likewise repeats the misinformed criticism that the "spiritual" overshadows the "sociopolitical" in Torrance's theology. In his words: "In a mirrored one-sidedness [to Sobrino's liberation Christology], Torrance rarely refers to liberation but speaks of the salvific effects achieved by Christ in overwhelmingly eternal and spiritual terms that cause him to miss the direct relevance of the cross to the temporal, material dimension of human life. Torrance employs a two-level view of reality in which the eternal, spiritual dimension trumps temporal, material reality, rendering insignificant the daily struggles of sociopolitical life" (241). It is telling that Hieb's bibliography includes none of Torrance's explicit essays on ethics, but even more significantly, that Hieb uncritically perpetuates Webster's criticism that misses Torrance's whole ethic of reconciliation of all things in Christ, which permeates his unitary and integrated theology. For a more informed assessment of Torrance's implicit social theology, see Eric Flett, *Persons, Powers, and Pluralities: Toward a Trinitarian Theology of Culture* (Eugene, OR: Pickwick, 2011). Also see Christopher Holmes, "'Renewal Through Union: Thomas F. Torrance on the New Basis of Ethics," *Participatio* Vol. 5: 45-55.

Torrance's entire theology as an ethic of reconciliation

The whole of Torrance's theological ethic is informed by what he calls a "soteriological suspension of ethics," alluding to and playing on Kierkegaard's "'teleological suspension of ethics' in the transition from a merely moral to a religious situation before God."[19] The Son acts personally and ontologically within the depths of our human existence in its estrangement, hurt, and violence in a vicarious way to assume and redeem our humanity.[20] Christ's humanity heals ours, including our moral selves and relations, our actions and motives as disciples of Christ. Following the lead of Kierkegaard as an incarnational theologian (not a textbook "existential philosopher"), Torrance treats "ethics" not as autonomous moral philosophy but as a matter of participation in Christ based on union with Christ. When Webster asserts that a doctrine of justification must "underline the primacy of the moral," of course in that sense Torrance did "neglect [or suspend] ethics," understood as human self-justification through autonomously defined presumed moral law. Torrance's viewpoint, however, favors *an account of justification that places human morality under the cross of Christ in order to reestablish a Christian ethic of faithful obedience and joyous gratitude to our God of reconciling grace.*

Underlying his Christian ethic is one of his oft-quoted biblical verses, Galatians 2.20 (as translated by Torrance): "I am crucified with Christ: nevertheless I live, yet not I but Christ lives in me; and the life which I now live in the flesh I live by faith, the faithfulness of the Son of God who loved me and gave himself for me." The vicarious humanity of Christ means that we may and must rely on his faithfulness to uphold and undergird *our humanity* (contra-Webster), including:

> all my human responses to God, for in Jesus Christ they are laid hold of, sanctified and informed by his vicarious life of obedience and response to the Father. They are in fact so indissolubly united to the life of Jesus Christ which he lived out among us and which he has offered to the Father, as arising out of our human being and nature that they are *our responses* toward the love of the Father poured out upon us through the mediation of the Son and in the unity of his Holy Spirit.[21]

---

19 Torrance, *The Trinitarian Faith* (Edinburgh: T. & T. Clark, 1988), 160, including n. 50.

20 Ibid., 156, 185.

21 Torrance, *The Mediation of Christ*, New Edition (Edinburgh: T & T Clark, 1992), 98 (emphasis Torrance's). Also see Andrew Purves' essay on Gal. 2:20 in *Participatio*: The

Christ's humanity, contra-Webster, *validates* our humanity as we live and act in union with him by his Spirit, which is to say, he grounds and establishes our fallen and faltering humanity as we participate in his covenant-keeping in our place and on our behalf. The vicarious humanity of Christ established St. Paul all the more in his own distinctive reality, so that more of Christ does not mean less of our humanity, as Webster assumes when he charges that Torrance "solely" or "exclusively" emphasizes the vicarious humanity of Christ. Webster's curious question, What "room is left" for genuine human activity?, relies on a zero-sum game. Christ's faithful and obedient humanity is precisely what makes room for our humanity and places a higher judgment on us when we neglect or refuse to be who we are and are becoming in him.

The vicarious humanity of Christ does not "threaten" or "absorb" humanity, as Webster seems forced to think, but in fact *frees us to be human!* Because "we rely wholly upon the vicarious faith of Christ and not upon ourselves even in the act of faith . . . we are really free to believe . . ."[22] Christ's vicarious faith makes both possible and necessary our act and life of faith. Christ's vicarious humanity, as we will see, sanctifies and informs and reorients our moral order, social reconciliation, and political responsibility, from moral conformity to a legal-religious code to a filial, trusting, loving obedience to God! *One can read the entirety of Torrance's body of work as a theology of reconciliation on all levels of life: personal, social, historical, political, and cosmic.*

The vicarious humanity of Christ suggests, not what Webster calls for as "policy-formation," but a filial ethic. Christ healed "the ontological depths" of our disobedient and alienated humanity and bent it back to "filial union with the Father" and "in indivisible oneness of agency with

---

Journal of the Thomas F. Torrance Fellowship, Supp. Vol. 2 (2013): 25-36. Elmer Colyer's excellent introduction, *How to Read T. F. Torrance: Understanding His Trinitarian & Scientific Theology* (Downers Grove, IL: IVP, 2001), is the source of the TFT translation of Gal. 2:20 (97). Colyer underscores that the vicarious humanity of Christ does not evacuate humanity of its response because "*all of grace* involves *all of humanity*" (118-9, emphasis added). I'm grateful to Professors Colyer and Purves for reading and making helpful comments on my essay.

22 Torrance, *The School of Faith: The Catechisms of the Reformed Church* (London: James Clarke, 1959), cix. Also see Christian Kettler's two volumes: *The God Who Believes: Faith, Doubt, and the Vicarious Humanity of Christ* (Eugene, OR: Wipf and Stock, 2005) and *The God Who Rejoices: Joy, Despair, and the Vicarious Humanity of Christ* (Eugene, OR: Wipf and Stock, 2010). I am grateful to Prof. Kettler for his many good comments and suggestions for my essay.

that of the Father and the Holy Spirit." In union with our brother Jesus, we are sons and daughters of the Father. Christ redeemed humanity "out of the depths of our actual existence through the incredible oneness which Christ forged with us in his vicarious humanity."[23] Because Jesus was God acting as one among us, God's reconciling work in the world is a reality and source of true humanity. The vicarious humanity of Christ bends back toward God our disobedient humanity so that we may truly and freely participate in Christ's humanity as we live and act in union with him.

Far from the vertical overshadowing the horizontal, as Fergusson charges, Christ's own humanity establishes the atonement in "our human existence" *because* it is anchored in God's own self-giving and reconciling being. The Spirit mediates Christ to us and us to Christ, so that we may actually participate in his vicarious and redemptive humanity. We live in union with Christ by the Spirit, for "Calvary and Pentecost belong integrally together."[24] Christ's cross and Spirit work together to bind us to Christ by God's grace, so that we may believe and live and act in union with him.

Torrance does resist a programmatic ethic of moral deeds and misdeeds, virtues and vices, for Christ's atoning work extends to all humanity and the whole creation, so "that the whole moral order had to be redeemed and be set on a new basis through the atonement." In Christ, we move from conformity to a moral code to a trusting and active obedience to the living God. The unity and distinction between us and God in Christ overcomes the "unbridgeable rift" in ourselves, given that God's moral ordering of human affairs since the Fall became an inexorable bondage to legalism. But Christ heals this very "unbridgeable rift between what we *are* and what we *ought* to be, for no matter how much we try to be what we ought to be we can never transcend that deep rift in ourselves."[25]

The atoning mediation of Christ entails, Torrance believes, "'a soteriological suspension of ethics' in the establishing of a new moral life that flows from grace in which external legal relation is replaced by inner filial relation to God the Father." By the presence and work of the Holy Spirit, he

---

[23] Torrance, "The Singularity of Christ and the Finality of the Cross: The Atonement and the Moral Order," in *Universalism and the Doctrine of Hell*, ed. Nigel M. de S. Cameron (Grand Rapids: Baker, 1992), 238-9.

[24] Ibid., 242-3. Also see Victor Shepherd's essay on the *homoousion* of the Holy Spirit in *Participatio: The Journal of the Thomas F. Torrance Fellowship*, Vol. 3 (2012): 108-24. I am indebted to Prof. Shepherd for his many incisive comments and suggestions for my essay.

[25] Ibid., 249-51.

The Soteriological Suspension of Ethics

continues, "this new life of ours in him is inwardly ruled by the indicatives of God's love rather than externally governed by the imperatives of the law."[26] For Torrance the merely ethical is legal, extrinsic, and lived out in a way that fails to recognize the person and work of Christ and of our reconciled relationship to God in him. Mere morality, for Torrance, must be superseded by the indicatives *and* imperatives of God's grace. In this way Christ fulfills "ethical obligations" or, as Torrance would say, humanity's covenant obligations to God, with his own filial obedience in which we now may and must participate by the Spirit as beloved children of our Father. Hence, contrary to the critics' contention, *we actually share in Christ's faith and obedience, and through his person and work we live humanly as his brothers and sisters and sons and daughters of his Father.*

Christ's atoning work is not merely moral or cognitive or legal but *ontological*:

> Here the ultimate ground of the moral order in God is no longer a detached imperative bearing down abstractly and externally upon us, for it has now been embodied once for all in the incarnate Person of the Lord Jesus Christ and takes the concrete and creative form of new righteousness that transcends the split between the is and the ought, the righteousness of our Lord's obedient Sonship in which our human relations with our Father in heaven have been healed and reconciled. We are now made through justification by grace to share in the righteousness of God in Christ. Thus we are made to live in union with him and in the communion of his Holy Spirit who sheds the love of God into our hearts, and informs our life with the very mind of Christ the obedient Son of the Father. This does not represent merely a conceptual change in our understanding of the moral order, but *a real ontological change resulting from the interlocking of incarnation and atonement in the depth and structure of our human existence and the translation of the Son/Father relation in Christ into the daily life of the children of God.*[27]

We are in fact new creatures in Christ, not merely conceptually but also ontologically; through the gift of the Spirit we may and must live and act, both graciously and dynamically, based on who we are and are becoming from now till the eschaton. All things are made new in Christ, which requires the *opposite* of what Webster unfortunately calls "excuses for inaction." The incarnate, crucified, and risen Christ, who has assumed and healed our humanity, calls us to follow him by participating in what he has done and

---

26 Ibid., 252-3.

27 Ibid., 254; emphasis added.

continues to do in the world; we act in union with Christ by the presence and power of the Spirit in service to God the Father on behalf of the world. Far from inaction, the Spirit calls us to take up our cross and follow Christ. To borrow a favorite phrase of J. B. Torrance (who with his brother T. F. Torrance affirms the vicarious humanity of Christ), *the unconditional indicatives of grace call for the unconditional obligations of grace.*

T. F. Torrance, in fundamental accord with Barth, affirms an actual change of humanity in Jesus Christ and through union with him. Over and against Webster's dichotomous framework, Jesus' humanity does not "threaten" or "absorb" or "invalidate" our humanity but validates our humanity on a "wholly new basis" in Christ:

> In Jesus Christ, God has intervened decisively in the moral impasse of humanity, doing a deed that humanity could not do itself. That impasse was not simply created by the inability of human beings to fulfill the holy demands of the law and justify themselves before God, but created by the very nature of the (moral) situation of man before God, so that it could not be solved from within itself as demanded by the law. Thus the intervention by God entailed a complete reversal of the moral situation and the setting of it on a wholly new basis ... as sheer gift of God's grace which is actualized in them as reality and truth.[28]

Christ's atoning work effects and announces "the great change and renewal of all things," "the whole of creation," and "*cosmic peace.*"[29] It is not merely a personal or private affair relegated to a so-called vertical plane of existence, which ignores and distorts his theological social ethic that extends in and throughout all strata of human life, including and transforming historical and horizontal existence. In Torrance's words:

> Hence we must think of the reconciling work of God in the cross, not only as once and for all completed and effected, but as travelling within and through our historical existence, as it were, as continually operative in reconciling intervention within history and all the affairs of humanity, and in the whole cosmos — *Immanuel,* God almighty with us in the midst of history, bearing all its sin and shame in his holy love, for he has already gathered it up upon himself.[30]

---

28 Torrance, *Incarnation: The Person and Life of Christ,* ed. R. T. Walker (Downers Grove, IL: IVP, 2008), 107.

29 Torrance, *Atonement: The Person and Work of Christ,* ed. R. T. Walker (Downers Grove IL: IVP, 2009), 168-9.

30 Ibid., 170.

The Soteriological Suspension of Ethics

All things are reconciled in Christ as "God's presence in sheer grace" breaks into the fallen cosmos, "so that not only human life but the whole of creation has been set on a wholly new basis."[31]

God's reconciling work penetrates and transforms the social spheres and horizontal domains of human life:

> For humanity, the redemption of the cross involves at the same time reconciliation of man with fellow man, of all men and women with each other, and particularly of Jew and Gentile, for the middle wall of partition has been broken down and God has made of them one new man in Christ Jesus. The word of the cross is not that all men and women are as a matter of fact at one with one another, but that such at-one-ment is achieved only in desperate and crucial action, through atonement in the death and resurrection of Christ. But because that has been finally achieved in Christ, the cross cuts clean across the divisions and barriers of the fashion of the world and resists them. It entails a judgement upon the old humanity of Babel and the proclamation of the new humanity in Christ Jesus which is necessarily one and universal. That becomes evident in the Christian church, whose function is *to live out the atonement in the world*, and that means to be in the flesh the bodily instrument of God's crucial intervention. And so the church becomes the sphere in which the great reconciliation, already wrought out in the body of Christ, is being realized among mankind, and the life and action of the church becomes sacramentally correlative to the life and passion of Christ Jesus.[32]

Reconciliation is a universal event, which the Spirit effects and actualizes as believers become "joined to Christ and therefore joined to a new universal humanity." Thus the crucified Christ breaks down "all the barriers of race and language" as he leads Christians "to proclaim reconciliation to all and to live it out, for it is by that same motion of universal reconciliation that he and she have themselves been redeemed in the cross."[33] Clearly our new status in Christ is a call to transforming action, not passive inaction! *We are to be who we already are and and are becoming in Christ.*

The risen and ascended humanity of Christ, contra-Fergusson, raises our humanity to a new status in him in order to continue by the Spirit Christ's ongoing work of reconciling the world. "The staggering thing

---

31 Ibid., 195.

32 Ibid., 199.

33 Ibid., 200.

about [the ascension]," Torrance insists, "is that the exaltation of human nature into the life of God does not mean the disappearance of man or the swallowing up of human and creaturely being in the infinite ocean of the divine being, but rather that human nature, while remaining creaturely and human, is yet exalted in Christ to share in God's life and glory." Christ's humanity does not swallow up our humanity, as characteristically occurs in non-biblical mysticism, just as Christ's divinity does not overtake his own humanity! Our new status in Christ does not function "as a flight from history, but precisely the reverse, as the invasion of history by the kingdom of Christ through the everlasting gospel."[34] *The vertical invades and redeems the horizontal*: "Participation in Christ carries with it participation in one another," Torrance clearly and emphatically proclaims, "and our common reconciliation with Christ carries with it reconciliation with one another."[35]

The Incarnation, Torrance proclaims, embodies God-in-person loving us and giving himself to us. The Incarnation is not a mere example of love (as it was for Arius and Harnack), but God's reconciling love and effectual action in light of the unique priority of the Incarnation (as it is for Athanasius, Barth, and Torrance). The Incarnation enacts, does not merely model, reconciliation.[36] In place of the Athanasian affirmation of the deity of Christ, however, "we see today the enormous emphasis on ethical and human values, on personality and social relations, in which man tries to find a foundation for his own feet."[37] Torrance suspends a Kantian ethic (or Webster's "primacy of the moral") as an autonomous human enterprise in search of self-justification — repeating and recapitulating Adam and Eve's Fall, which replaced God's concrete command with the abstract moral philosophy of the good, true, and beautiful.

Torrance advocates an Athanasian-Trinitarian-ontological ethic in continuity with the ancient and orthodox faith over and against an Arian-unitarian-moralistic view of redemption:

> If Jesus Christ is only morally related to God himself, then the best he can be is a kind of moral Leader who through his own example in love and righteousness points us to a better moral relationship with the heavenly Father . . . The Church then becomes little more than a way of gathering people together on moral grounds or

---

34 Ibid., 294-6.

35 Ibid., 375.

36 Torrance, *The Doctrine of Jesus Christ* (Eugene, OR: Wipf and Stock, 2002), 85-6.

37 Ibid, 243.

The Soteriological Suspension of Ethics

socio-political issues . . . But if Jesus Christ is God the Creator himself become incarnate among us, he saves and heals by opening up the dark, twisted depths of our human being and cleansing, reconciling and recreating us from within the very foundations of our existence.[38]

In the Incarnation, the Son assumes both our human nature as created and as fallen, healing what he has assumed as a prolepsis of our humanity in the crucified, risen, ascended, and coming humanity of Christ. The Arian view, however, more simply and superficially relies on a doctrine of human self-justification:

> Thus there has opened up a deep gap in our relations with God and with one another which we cannot bridge. . . . The human heart is so desperately wicked that it cunningly takes advantage of the hiatus between what we are and what we ought to be in order to latch on to the patterns and structures of moral behavior required of us, so that under the image of what is good and right it masks or even fortifies its evil intentions. Such is the self-deception of our human heart and the depravity of our self-will that we seek to justify ourselves before God and our neighbors . . .[39]

Jesus Christ, however, "became the humanising Man who constitutes among us the creative source for the humanising of mankind," the true healing, restoring, and establishing of human morality and social existence from the perspective of an Athanasian vs. Arian social ethic.

> Now if from this perspective, in light of the fact that as the Mediator between God and man Jesus Christ is the personalising Person and the humanizing man, we look back at the doctrine of the Church, we may be able to see more clearly why the Church is not merely a society of individuals gathered together on moral grounds and externally connected with one another through common ethical ideals, for there is no way through external organization to effect personalizing or humanizing of people in society or therefore of transforming human social relations. But that is precisely what takes place through the ontological reconciliation with God effected in the Mediation of Christ which binds the Church to Christ as his Body. Through union and communion with Christ human society may be transmuted into a Christian community in which inter-personal relations are

---

38 Torrance, *Mediation of Christ*, 61-2.

39 Ibid., 71.

healed and restored in the Person of the Mediator, and in which interrelations between human beings are constantly renewed and sustained through the humanizing activity of Christ Jesus, the one Man in whom and through whom as Mediator between God and man they may be reconciled to one another within the ontological and social structures of their existence. . . . *The very same message applies to human society, for in virtue of what takes place in the Church through corporate union and communion with Jesus Christ as his Body, the promise of transformation and renewal of all human social structures is held out in the Gospel, when Society may at last be transmuted into a community of love centring in and sustained by the personalizing and humanizing presence of the Mediator.*"[40]

Reconciliation is a social, historical, and even cosmic — not merely a private — affair, but this is a wholly other reality based on an Athanasian-ontological, rather than an Arian-moralistic, view of things. God's humanity sanctifies and humanizes our humanity in its vertical and horizontal, cosmic and societal dimensions, contrary to the critics who have missed this socio-ethical-political theme in Torrance's theology.

Very far from a private or vertical ethic — and in precisely the opposite direction! — Christ has even redeemed the space-time structures of the cosmos, the actual conditions of our humanity and all that supports human existence:

> [I]t is necessary to see that the resurrection means the redemption of space and time, for space and time are not abrogated or transcended. Rather are they healed and restored, just as our being is healed and restored through the resurrection. Of course we cannot separate our being from space and time for space and time are conditions and functions of created existence and the bearers of its order. The healing and restoring of our being carries with it the healing, restoring, reorganizing and transforming of the space and time in which we now live our lives in relation to one another and to God.[41]

Christ has redeemed us from "the *nomistic form of human existence* that is thrown into sharp relief by justification," so that fallen humanity is no longer enslaved to ethical self-justification, given the gap between the is and ought that plagues our attempts to do good on our own and without God. We may now participate in "the life-giving New Man" by his Spirit

---

40 Ibid., 72; emphasis added.
41 Torrance, *Space, Time and Resurrection* (Grands Rapids: Eerdmans, 1976), 90-1.

and through his body the Church, both to proclaim and to practice the reality of reconciliation in Christ within this fallen world.[42] God in Christ by the Spirit has moved human moral activity out of the sphere and business of legalistic moral self-promotion into the sphere of God's Kingdom, wherein our standing with God is both *gift* (with gratitude to the covenant faithfulness of the Son whose humanity includes and reorients ours) and *task* (but not a Kantian moral autonomy that reduces true religion to mere ethics). In Christ, we may and must love God from the heart, obey him throughout all of life, and love all our neighbors, both near and afar, as our brothers and sisters in God's Kingdom.

Torrance's trinitarian-incarnational ethic assumes and announces an inter-relationship of faith and godliness: of worship, behavior, and thought. As he writes,

> An outstanding mark of the Nicene approach was its association of faith with 'piety' or 'godliness' . . . that is, with a mode of worship, behavior and thought that was devout and worthy of God the Father, the Son, and the Holy Spirit. This was a distinctively Christian way of life in which the seal of the Holy Trinity was indelibly stamped upon the mind . . . of the Church.[43]

The Creator is the Redeemer, who intervenes in human affairs, binds and reconciles the whole universe in himself, and grants a contingent freedom to participate in his own freedom — all dependent upon the genuine humanity of the Son in his oneness of being and agency with his Father.[44] The Spirit of Christ actualizes within the Church the whole life and ministry, person and work of Christ, "healing and restoring and deepening human personal being" as "*personalised persons,*" both "in relation to God and in relation to one another." The Spirit "actualises among us the self-giving of God to us in his Son, and resonates and makes fruitful within us the intervening, atoning and intercessory activity of God on our behalf."[45]

Christ's reconciling work comports better with the "real participation" theology of Paul, Athanasius, Barth, and Torrance more so than the mere "moral resemblance" view of Arius, Kant, and Harnack. Social reconciliation *under the cross of Christ and grounded in the very being and life of God*

---

42 Ibid., 96-9.
43 *Trinitarian Faith*, 17.
44 Ibid., 91, 107, 137ff.
45 Ibid., 190, 230, 249.

himself exposes the moral order itself for leading us back into legalistic moralism as human agents before God, and so it too needs God's gracious healing in Christ. Torrance understands Christ's atoning work operating on "the inner ontological relations" between Christ and God and between Christ and humankind, which

> implies that the very basis for a merely moral or legal account of atonement is itself part of the actual state of affairs between man and God that needs to be set right. The moral relations that obtain in our fallen world have to do with the gap between what we are and what we ought to be, but it is that very gap that needs to be healed, for even what we call 'good', in fulfillment of what we ought to do, needs to be cleansed by the blood of Christ. . . . The inexplicable fact that God in Christ has actually taken our place, tells us that the whole moral order itself as we know it in this world needed to be redeemed and set on a new basis, but that is what the justifying act of God in the sacrifice of Christ was about. . . . Such is the utterly radical nature of the atoning mediation perfected in Christ, which is to be grasped, as far as it may, not in the light of abstract moral principle, but only in the light of what he has actually done in penetrating into the dark depths of our twisted human existence and restoring us to union and communion with God in and through himself. In this interlocking of incarnation and atonement, and indeed of creation and redemption, there took place what might be called a 'soteriological suspension of ethics' in order to reground the whole moral order in God himself.[46]

The "suspension" of ethics, for Torrance, is not a temporary disruption of human activity but a permanent alteration, redemption, and transformation of the very categories of moral decision-making and action in God's gracious action in Christ.

While Torrance discusses an "epistemological inversion" required for our knowledge of God, which is based on God's self-revelation rather than our mythological projections,[47] *mutatis mutandis* we will speak of a related

---

46 Ibid., 160-1. For a discussion of Torrance's understanding of "ontological" as "onto-relational" (and thus inherently ethical), see Gary Deddo, "The realist and onto-relational Frame of T. F. Torrance's Incarnational and Trinitarian Theology," *Theology in Scotland* (Vol. XVI, 2011), 105-33.

47 Torrance writes, "Within the sphere of divine revelation an *epistemological inversion* takes place in our knowing of God, for what is primary is his knowing of us, not our knowing of him." See *The Christian Doctrine of God, One Being Three Persons* (Edinburgh: T&T Clark, 1996), 105.

ethical inversion. In place of autonomous morality arising from a center out of ourselves, Christ reconciles us to our neighbors by relating us to God, who is personal, dynamic, and relational. "While the being of God is not to be understood as constituted by his relation to others," writes Torrance, "that free outward flowing of his Being in gratuitous love toward and for others reveals to us something of the inmost nature of God's being . . ."[48] In fundamental agreement with Barth (irrespective of measured volume of output on "ethics"!), Torrance insists that we have no life based in our autonomous and self-justifying selves but only in Christ:

> Thus in living out to the full in our humanity the relation of the Son to the Father, and therefore in bringing the Father into direct and immediate relation with the whole of our human life, Jesus Christ was the perfect man perfectly reflecting the glory of God, but as such and precisely as such, the whole course of Christ's perfect human life on earth was identical with the whole course of the Father's action toward mankind.[49]

Christ as the Son of the Father in the presence and power of the Spirit overcomes the human split between the *is* and the *ought*. Torrance's ethic is not moralistic or legalistic but filial! Because Christ is our brother, we are God's children. Christ's true humanity, God as one among us, is the basis of our human-ethical activity in and through the Church. Torrance does indeed have a "moral ontology," which however is rooted in our filial relationship with Christ in, by, and through the Spirit in relationship to God. Contra-Webster, Torrance upholds a clear and intrinsic connection between both Christ's person and work and human being and activity as service in Jesus Christ squarely situated in the world. The "intrinsic connexion" between Christ and us is that Christ's obedience to the Father quickens our faith-wrought love, gratitude, and obedience.

Torrance's Christian ethic based on the atoning work of Christ, not on the self-justifying action of the sinner

Torrance's trinitarian-incarnational ethic begins with a foundational axiom from his essay "The Eclipse of God": Jesus Christ alone frees us to love God and our neighbors by sharing in his life and our renewed and transformed

---

48 Ibid., 123-4.

49 Torrance, *Incarnation*, 126.

humanity, "not out of a centre in ourselves . . ." Furthermore, "It is only in and through Jesus Christ that man's eclipse of God can come to an end and he can emerge again out of darkness into light," which means "to hear a Word coming to him from beyond which he could never tell to himself."[50]

Torrance continues his trinitarian-incarnational ethic in his essay "Cheap and Costly Grace": *Christus pro me* frees us from the autonomous ethical enterprise and refers us back "to the objective intervention of God in Christ, a saving act independent of man himself by which he is liberated even from himself, for there is nothing that man can do by way of knowledge or decision or believing that can deliver him from his in-turned, self-centred self."[51] To quote Torrance at length from this critical essay,

> Let us consider then what is involved in justification by Christ alone. It means that it is Christ, and not we ourselves, who puts us in the right and truth of God, so that He becomes the center of reference in all our thought and action, the determinative point in our relations with God and man to which everything else is made to refer for verification or justification. But what a disturbance in the field of our personal relations that is bound to create! Many years ago when I read a well-known book on *The Elements of Moral Theology* I was astonished to find that Jesus Christ hardly came into it at all. He had been thrust into a corner where He could hardly be noticed, while the ethical and indeed the casuistical concern dominated the whole picture. But what emerged was an ethic that was fundamentally continuous with their ordinary natural existence and was essentially formal. How different altogether, I thought, was the ethical disturbance that attended the teaching and actions of Jesus or the upheaval that broke in upon contemporary society and law when He proclaimed the absolutes of the Kingdom of God, and summoned people to radical obedience . . . What the Gospel of Jesus proclaims is that God Himself has stepped into our situation and made Himself responsible for us in a way that sets our life on a wholly new basis.[52]

Jesus healed our self-willed inner being, so that we may be truly and fully responsible for moral action. Therefore, Torrance's Christian ethic is an evangelical ethic:

---

50 Torrance, *God and Rationality* (London: Oxford, 1971), 54-5.
51 Ibid., 58-9.
52 Ibid., 60-2.

The Soteriological Suspension of Ethics

> Jesus Christ has come to lift man out of that predicament in which even when he has done all that it is his duty to do . . . he can never overtake the ethical 'ought' . . . . [I]n Jesus Christ God has already taken a decision about our existence and destiny in which He has set us on the ground of His pure grace where we are really free for spontaneous ethical decisions toward God and toward men. This means that the decision to which man is summoned in the *kerygma* of Jesus is one that reposes upon the prior and objective decision that He has taken on our behalf and which He announces to us freely and unconditionally.[53]

Justification by Christ alone suggests a soteriological suspension and categorical transformation of self-justifying ethics:

> God Himself has intervened in our ethical predicament where our free-will is our self-will and where we are unable to extricate ourselves from the vicious moral circle created by our self-will, in order to be selflessly free for God or for our neighbor in love. It means that God has interacted with our world in a series of decisive events within our historical and moral existence in which He has emancipated us from the thraldom of our own failure and redeemed us from the curse of the law that held us in such bitter bondage to ourselves that we are now free to engage in obedience to God's will without secondary motives, but also so free from concern for ourselves and our own self-understanding that we may love both God and our neighbour objectively for their own sakes. It is thus that justification involves us in a profound moral revolution and sets all our ethical relations on a new basis, but it happens only when Christ occupies the objective center of human existence and all things are mediated through His grace.[54]

Against his critics, *Torrance's theological ethic reposes on the interrelationship of Incarnation and Atonement*. "Apart from Christ's incarnational union with us and our union with Christ on that ontological basis," he warns, "justification degenerates into only an empty moral relation."[55] Christ is the very ground and grammar of theology, salvation, and ethics. Torrance relies upon Athanasius vs. Arius not only for his theology but also for his ethics!

---

53   Ibid., 62.
54   Ibid., 62-3.
55   Ibid., 64-5.

Torrance's recurrent call for an "epistemological inversion" suggests an ethical correlate that turns programs and human projects (or "policy-formation," as Webster wishes) on their head:

> By pouring forth upon men unconditional love, by extending freely to all without exception total forgiveness, by accepting men purely on the ground of the divine grace, Jesus became the center of a volcanic disturbance in human existence, for He not only claimed the whole of man's existence for God but exposed the hollowness of the foundations upon which man tries to establish himself before God.[56]

An autonomous ethic, to sharpen the point, suggests a sinful self-reliance, which indicates that Torrance stands in basic continuity both with Barth and with Bonhoeffer too:

> That is to say, are we to learn how to live without God, without prayer, without the supernatural, without any belief in or thought of the interaction of God with our world? If so, does this not really mean that we are thrown back fully and finally upon ourselves? . . . Bonhoeffer starts, like Barth, from the fundamental principle of the justification of the sinner by grace alone which makes a man really free for God and his brothers, for it sets his life on a foundation other than himself where he is sustained by a power other than his own. Justification by grace alone removes from us all false props, all reliance upon external authorities, and all refuge in worldly securities, and throws us not upon ourselves but upon the pure act of God in His unconditional love, so that the ethical and the religious life are lived exclusively from a centre in Jesus Christ.[57]

Torrance clearly and unequivocally aligns himself with Dietrich Bonhoeffer's theological ethic (which is to say, Karl Barth too):

> Christian ethic is ontologically structured in Jesus Christ and therefore participates in and through Him in His victory over the dualism between two separate spheres. It is because he took so seriously the incarnation of the Son of God in the space and time of this world that he insisted 'that there is no real possibility of being a Christian outside the reality of this world and that there is no real worldly existence outside the reality of Jesus Christ'. There is no place therefore to which the Christian can withdraw from the

---

56 Ibid., 66.
57 Ibid., 76.

The Soteriological Suspension of Ethics

world; rather must he learn to live out the reality of Christ within it, for it is in that world that He the Son of God made our reality His own, and made His reality ours.[58]

In "The Word of God and the Response of Man" (which Webster rightly dubbed as "monumental," even while neglecting its significance for ethics):

> We recall that in Jesus Christ the Word of God has established reciprocity with us in the conditions, structures and limitations of our creaturely existence and within the alienation, disorder and disintegration of our human being where we are subject to the wasting power of evil and the divine judgement upon it, in order to lay hold of our world and sustain it from below, to recreate its relation to the Creator and realize its true response to Him as God and Father of all. That is to say, in Jesus Christ the transcendent Rationality of God has planted itself within the created order where its bounds, structures and connections break down under the negation of evil, in order to reintegrate spiritual and physical existence by setting up its own law within it, and restore it to wholeness and integrity in the form, as it were, of a meeting of the Rationality of God with itself in the midst of estranged existence and in the depths of its disorder. In this way, the incarnation has affected the whole creation, confirming the primordial act of the Word in conferring order and rationality upon it.[59]

Torrance, not surprisingly, upholds a unitary or holistic view of Christian service in and through Christ on behalf of all humanity and creation: "We cannot hold apart the ministry of love from the activity of science, nor may we pursue our scientific exploration of the universe except in obedience to the God of love." He continues:

> If we are to follow this Jesus in the modern world we must surely learn how to apply scientific knowledge and method to such terrible problems as hunger, poverty, and want, without falling into the temptation to build up power-structures of our own, through ecclesiastical prestige, social success or political instrumentality, in order to make our ministry of compassion effective within the power-structures of the world, for then we would contract out of Christian service as *service* and betray the weakness of Jesus. On the other hand, if we are to engage in scientific exploration of the universe, in response to the Word of God incarnate in Jesus Christ by whom it was

---

58 Ibid., 78.

59 Torrance, *Gospel, Church, and Ministry* (Eugene, OR: Wipf and Stock, 2012), 163.

made, we must learn to respect the nature of all created things, using pure science to bring their mute rationality into such articulation that the praises of the Creator may resound throughout the whole universe, without falling into the temptation to exploit nature through an instrumentalist science in the interest of our own self-aggrandizement and lust for power, for then also would we contract out of Christian service as service and sin against the hiddenness of Jesus in the world. No doubt, the created rationalities of word and number are very different, as different as the world of persons and the world of things, but they both go back to the same source in the transcendent Rationality of God and they are both brought together in the incarnation of God's Word in Jesus Christ, for they are upheld and sustained by Him. Therefore our service in the realm of word and our service in the realm of number must be co-ordinated through Jesus Christ in our common response to the love of God.[60]

Torrance's essays in *Gospel, Church, and Ministry* offer a personal glimpse of the man who was first and foremost a minister of the Gospel — and perhaps Webster is right after all that he was not an "ethicist" because he was not a dualist! Regarding parish ministry, Torrance did not separate proclamation of the Gospel and pastoral visitation, and likewise later, he could not separate his theology lectures and the personal power of the Gospel. For example, Torrance had weekly dinner and discussion with his parishioners, who considerably helped him relate the Gospel to daily life and work. In a monthly study with parishioners of the Sermon on the Mount, one parishioner raised his farm workers' salaries above the government standard, which increased the prosperity both of the farmer and his workers.[61] Service in Jesus Christ by his body the Church, exceeds, not displaces, government standards and programs.

When the Church becomes merged with society and culture, its "mild form of Christianity" leaves it with no message to the modern world. The Church should not identify herself with any social order or political regime, "far less with the 'status quo.'"

> The Church can only be the Christian Church when she is ever on the move, always campaigning, always militant, aggressive, revolutionary. . . . to turn the whole order of State and society, national and international, upside down. . . . By throwing the social environment into ferment and upheaval, by an aggressive

---

60 Ibid., 163-4.
61 Ibid., 35, 50.

> evangelism with the faith that rebels against all wrong and evil, and by a new machinery through which her voice will be heard in the councils of the nation as never before, the Church will press toward a new order. Whenever there is evil in the industrial and economic order, in the political or international sphere so in the social fabric of ordinary life, the Church must press home the claims of the Christian gospel and ethic. . . . [T]he great task of the Church is the redemption of the world and not a comfortable life in little, religious churches and communities.[62]

The Church has a unique existence, message, and function, which excludes a merger or identification with society, or a confusion of Christianity as Christendom, or an equation of moral or civic life with the Christian life. The Church does have a worldly form, and its methods and organization should translate the Gospel to society, "through which she can have a purchase upon the State"![63]

The Church is both conservative and revolutionary (perhaps contrary to critics' view of Torrance's political ethic as the former but not the latter?): the servant of the living God, not to uphold and justify the status quo but to take initiative in society to check the authoritarian State. So A: The Church must recover her distinctiveness and believe again that the proclamation of the gospel is her primary task, refusing to identify with any social system or political program and especially taking offensive action against the status quo. And B: The Church must overhaul its organizational forms and outmoded methods, especially ad hoc measures that are out of step with modern, business-like finance.[64] The Church witnesses to the gospel as it advances "the claims of the Christian gospel and ethic" in all spheres of life: personal, social, industrial, economic, political, and international. For God is ushering in a new order of "peace and brotherly relations on the basis of the Christian ethic" — checking for example the basic human tendency toward a will to power or a focus upon ourselves, and instead presenting to society the Christ who came as a ransom for many to redeem the world.[65]

Torrance's Athanasian vs. Arian love-ethic proclaims that "God is the great householder who has come to take control of his own house and family and order it according to his love," for "in the whole human life of Jesus the

---

62 Ibid., 43.
63 Ibid., 75 6.
64 Ibid., 76-81.
65 Ibid, 81-4.

order of creation has been restored." The Christian Church participates in the redeemed order of humanity and creation in Jesus Christ, who took the form of a Servant — "not simply an imitation of his obedience but a fulfilling of God's will through participation in Christ's obedience" by the person and power of the Spirit.[66] Again, contra Webster's early essays that pit imitation against participation, participation in Christ does not pose a false dichotomy over and against an imitation of Christ, even though for Torrance the former precedes and includes the latter.

Christian service, for Torrance, is not an optional matter: "The great characteristic of all Christian service or *diakonia* is that while it is certainly fulfilled under the constraint of the love of Christ it is a service *commanded* by him and laid by him as a *task* upon every baptized member of his body." He continues, again in complete agreement with Barth: "The content of the commandment and the content of the service in obedience to it derive from the self-giving of God himself in Jesus Christ the Lord. He gives what he commands and commands what he gives. He commands a service of love, and he gives the love that empowers that service."[67] Torrance's ethic, following Barth (and contra-Webster), is one of obedience to a person and not adherence to "the primacy of the moral."

Human mercy mirrors and participates in the mercy of God himself: "It is the very property of God's nature to be merciful, and in mercy it is that nature that he has come to share with men and women in Jesus, that they, too, may be merciful as he is merciful."[68] Reminiscent of Matt. 25 (and Calvin), Torrance proclaims his unitary theological ethic:

> Hence Christ is to be found wherever there is sickness or hunger or thirst or nakedness or imprisonment, for he has stationed himself in the concrete actualities of human life where the bounds and structures of existence break down under the onslaught of disease and want, sin and guilt, death and judgement, in order that he may serve man in re-creating his relation to God and realizing his response to the divine mercy. It is thus that Jesus Christ mediates in himself the healing reconciliation of God with man and man with God in the form, as it were, of a meeting of himself with himself in the depths of human need.[69]

---

66 Ibid., 94-7.
67 Ibid., 140-2.
68 Ibid., 145.
69 Ibid., 150.

The Soteriological Suspension of Ethics

> The Church cannot be in Christ without being in him as he is proclaimed to men in their need and without being in him as he encounters us in and behind the existence of every man in his need. Nor can the Church be recognized as his except in that meeting of Christ with himself in the depth of human misery, where Christ clothed with his gospel meets Christ clothed with the desperate need and plight of men.[70]

The Church must resist a two-fold temptation. First is the enticement to use worldly power to secure success, "not only to institutionalize its service of the divine mercy but to build up power structures of its own." The Church should nonetheless support on behalf of the poor and hungry "scientific methods in the production and distribution of goods from the vast wealth with which God has endowed the earth." Second is the allurement of retreat into a spiritual ministry of forgiveness, which concedes corporate responsibility to the State for the betterment of human welfare. This second temptation, like the first, means "the Church would decline the burden of human need at its sharpest point and deflect the real force of Christian witness, and so run away from the agony of being merciful as God is merciful."[71]

While Torrance's Christian ethic is not primarily moral or political — and perhaps its greatest strength is its service as a counterpoint to the many politicized theologies of our day! — it is centered on the Church's service to God in the world. And Christ calls his Church to a three-fold ministry of service to: (1) believe in intercessory prayer as a direct reliance upon God and as a direct engagement with the world, rather than "frantic attempts" to make its ministry and message relevant, powerful, and successful; (2) practice evangelistic and suffering witness on behalf of all people in their estrangement and separation and alienation from God; and (3) live the reconciled life first and foremost by healing its own internal divisions, which mirror the divisive forces of evil in the world, so that it may "live out in the midst of a broken and divided humanity the reconciled life of the one unbroken Body of Jesus Christ — that is *diakonia*."[72]

One preeminent moral issue for the one body of Christ is what Torrance boldly calls an "'apartheid' between different churches"![73]

---

70 Ibid., 151.
71 Ibid., 154-5.
72 Ibid., 160.
73 Ibid., 179.

> Until the Christian Church heals within itself the division between the service of Jesus Christ clothed with his gospel and the service of Christ clothed with the need and affliction of men, and until it translates its communion in the body and blood of Christ into the unity of its own historical existence in the flesh, it can hardly expect the world to believe, for its *diakonia* would lack elemental integrity. But *diakonia* in which believing active intercession, bold unashamed witness, and the reconciled life are all restored in the mission of the Church will surely be the service with which Jesus Christ is well pleased, for that is the *diakonia* which he has commanded of us and which he has appointed as the mirror through which he reflects before the world his own image in the form of a Servant.[74]

Holy Communion, for example, is a diaconal ministry of "distribution of goods from the Lord's Table which presupposes a complex practice in which the Lord's Supper and the Love-feast, the Eucharist and the Agape, and the evangelical mission of the Church, were closely bound together." In fact, as Torrance comments and commends, deacons of the Early Church distributed the goods or gifts from the Lord's Table to the poor.[75] Perhaps Torrance would object to Holy Communion in the church sanctuary with linen cloth covering the altar or Lord's Table, dualistically separated from a soup kitchen on bare tables in the church's basement?[76] Christ distributes food and drink through his body to the poor and hungry and homeless, among whom Christ himself dwells and ministers. Perhaps churches should display in these food distribution centers sacramental symbols, such as the Lord's Table accompanied by Jesus' words in Matt. 25:35-40 [NEB]: "For when I was hungry, you gave me food; when I was thirsty, you gave me drink; when I was a stranger, you took me into your home; when naked you clothed me; when I was ill you came to my help; when in prison you visited me . . . I tell you this: anything you did for one of my brothers here, however humble, you did for me.'"

---

74 Ibid., 161.

75 Ibid., 199.

76 The last chapter of this book, "Ray S. Anderson's Doctrine of Humanity as a Contribution to a Theology of Culture: A Case Study Approach," will address the dualism of worship on Sunday separated from AA meetings on Saturday, drawing upon TFT's theological ethic via his student Ray Anderson. The upshot of the essay is that alcoholics need the living God, as the founders of AA believed and experienced, not just a "higher power," which was a pragmatic compromise that capitulated to the religious pluralism of our culture.

The Soteriological Suspension of Ethics

Jesus' words in Matt. 11:27b-30 [NEB] are also crucial for Torrance: "Everything is entrusted to me by my Father; and no one knows the Son but the Father, and no one knows the Father but the Son and those to whom the Son may choose to reveal him. Come unto me, all whose work is hard, whose load is heavy; and I will give you relief. Bend your necks to my yoke, and learn from me, for I am gentle and humble-hearted; and your souls will find relief. For my yoke is good to bear, my load is light." So the work of Christ is the work of the Father, in whom we participate by the power and presence of the Spirit. Following Christ in discipleship, which involves "ethics" too, means being where Christ is on behalf of the poor and hungry and thirsty and needy. For that is where we ourselves meet Christ, and invite those whom we encounter in the presence of Christ in mutual need of God's grace given to us and for us.

The early Church helped transform society, not by political and ideological programs or theologies of liberation, but by being faithful to the gospel of God's intervention, redemption, and transformation of our human and social existence. The Church's ministry and mission is the proclamation of the Word and pastoral visitation and counsel "to people as *persons*" — not as "pawns of politicians" or secular psychology and counseling as a replacement of the personal ministry of the Word."[77] Christ has redeemed the whole of human existence as God among us in our place and on our behalf.

Contrary to Webster, Christ "does not override our humanity but completes, perfects, and establishes it," especially in light "of bringing Christian understanding of the personal relations within the Holy Trinity to bear upon social relations and structures..."[78] The vicarious humanity of Christ, very far from "invalidating" human being and agency, does just the opposite. Christ assumes, heals, and sanctifies our humanity, placing "all our human life and activity before God," "under the judgment of the cross ... our goodness as well as our badness," and redeeming and reorienting the ontological depths of our humanity through his true humanity.[79] Torrance does indeed affirm an intrinsic and integrated relationship between what Christ has done as one among us, in our place and on our behalf, creating a new and transformed basis for human morality,

---

77 Ibid., 162-6, 170.

78 Torrance, *Preaching Christ Today: The Gospel and Scientific Thinking* (Grand Rapids, Eerdmans, 1994), 13, 26.

79 Ibid., 30, 35, 59.

interpersonal relations, social structures, and the created order. While one might disagree with his specific conclusions on moral and social issues, the critics themselves have neglected and ignored his implicit and explicit Christian theological ethic.

Torrance's views on five social-ethical issues

The following issues illustrate how Torrance has addressed moral matters that are both personal and social (as if one could separate human issues in such dualistic fashion). His larger point about the soteriological suspension of ethics underscores his unitary framework of knowledge, but this foundation did not prevent him from also addressing concrete ethical issues (whether or not one agrees with his conclusions). The following are examples of how he addressed them and suggest how he would address other moral matters. As his mentor, Barth, said when asked if he would complete *Church Dogmatics*: If you have read what I have written, you will know where I was going! The same could be said of Torrance's treatment of ethics: although occasional, they are indicative of how Torrance discussed Christ's concrete call to follow him in ministry and service.

> The call and **ordination of women** for the ministry of the Gospel, for Torrance, is based on an evangelical egalitarianism that presupposes the "radical change" effected in Christ — i.e., "the old divisions in the fallen world have been overcome in Christ and in his Body the Church," a reversal and "healing of any divisive relation between male and female due to the curse imposed upon them at the fall" (Gen. 3:16).[80]

Torrance argues concretely and forcefully:

> Thus any preeminence of the male sex or any vaunted superiority of man over woman was decisively set aside at the very inauguration of the new creation brought about by the incarnation. In Jesus Christ the order of redemption has intersected the order of creation and set it upon a new basis altogether. Henceforth the full equality of man and woman is a divine ordinance that applies to all the behavior and activity of 'the new man' in Christ, and so to the entire life and mission of the Church as the Body of Christ in the world ...[81]

---

80 Torrance, *The Ministry of Women* (Edinburgh: Handsel Press, 1992), 3-5.
81 Ibid., 5.

The Soteriological Suspension of Ethics

> [I]n view of this representative and substitutionary nature of the sacrifice of Christ, to insist that only a man, or a male, can rightly celebrate the Eucharist on the ground that only a male can represent Christ, would be to sin against the blood of Christ, for it would discount the substitutionary aspect of the atonement. At the altar the minister or priest acts faithfully in the name of Christ, the incarnate Saviour, only as he lets himself be displaced by Christ, and so fulfils his proper ministerial representation of Christ at the Eucharist in the form of a relation 'not I but Christ,' in which his own self, let alone his male nature, does not come into the reckoning at all. In the very act of celebration his own self is, as it were, withdrawn from the scene.[82]

While Torrance took this more progressive theological view on women's ordination, he also upheld a traditional theological view of **God-language** — and whether or not one agrees with him, once again, these issues illustrate his concern for concrete personal and social issues:

> Thus the act of God's self-revealing to us takes our human speaking, hearing, and knowing into its concrete realization within God's personal interrelation with us and so there is necessarily included within it an *anthropomorphic* component. It cannot be stressed too much that this is not an anthropomorphic element which is generated by any independent act of knowing or conceiving of God on our part, but one that arises in the self-determination of God's being toward us, in his creating us for fellowship with himself, in his establishing personal relations between us and himself, and in his making himself known to us within those relations. As such, the anthropomorphic component is to be understood not in terms of some cultural inheritance from the past that we may replace as we choose, but in terms of what God himself has adapted and defined in his unique self-revealing to us. It is not, therefore, something defined by what we human beings are of ourselves and projected by us onto God in our conceiving of him.... Accordingly, human fatherhood may not be used as a standard by which to judge divine Fatherhood, for there is strictly no comparison between human fatherhood and divine Fatherhood any more than there is between human being and divine Being.[83]

---

82 Ibid., 12.

83 Torrance, "The Christian Apprehension of God the Father," in *Speaking the Christian God: The Holy Trinity and the Challenge of Feminism*, ed. A. Kimel (Grand Rapids: Eerdmans, 1992), 124, 129-30.

Torrance borrows from Athanasius: "It would be more godly and true (or accurate) to signify God from the Son and call him Father, than to name God from his works alone and call him Unoriginate," which would be based on a "center in ourselves" rather than a "center in God." The trinitarian formula expresses God's unique and personal self-revelation, which excludes generic or unitarian substitutes such as "Creator, Redeemer, and Sustainer." Only the blessed Trinity "conveys the truth of God's intrinsically *personal, interpersonal,* and *personalizing* being" — over and against impersonal conceptions based on "the personification and deification of our own desires and ideals" or "submerged in waves of sociocultural secularization in which the souls of men, women, and children are easily and quickly drowned."[84]

Ray Anderson, student of Torrance, writes in the same volume:

> The historical particularity — and scandal — of the incarnation of God begins with the man Jesus. But rather than *divinizing* the male at the expense of the female, the incarnation *humanizes* both male and female by bringing their biological and gender differentiation under judgment for the sake of revealing the true nature of God and the true status of humanity as created in the divine image, male and female.[85]

Torrance's argument against **abortion** (in most cases, as long as exceptions do not become norms) begins with a goal to "keep medicine to *the art of healing human persons,* i.e. of persons regarded as a unity of physical and spiritual realities," "beyond its merely physical or biological existence," for the unborn child is *"body of his soul and soul of his body."* "The human being is an integrated whole . . . an *embodied soul* and a *besouled body"* — once again in basic agreement with Barth. This unitary human being is essentially male and female, male or female, as the "basic feature of humanity" — so sex "may not be reduced to its physical and biological aspects," which would perpetuate the "animalisation of sex" so prevalent in modern society.[86] Contrawise, Torrance writes on marriage, "The basic unit of creation is not the individual human being, male or female, but man

---

84 Ibid., 132-3, 141-3.

85 Anderson, "The Incarnation of God in Feminist Christology: A Theological Critique," Ibid., 308-9.

86 Torrance, *The Soul and Person of the Unborn Child* (Edinburgh: Handsel Press, 1999), 4, 7-8.

and woman joined together as one," which is grounded in God's creative and redemptive work.[87]

Thus, "the embryonic child, male or female, is an embodied soul and a besouled body, and as such is already, not a potential, but an incipient person," which Torrance views as "from the moment of conception," which provides support from modern science that he or she is "genetically complete." He does acknowledge "that difficult circumstances arise in which exception is called for in the prohibition of abortion," but in a relativistic society exceptions are turned into rules, which with Michael Polanyi he calls a "moral inversion." "[T]he unborn-child in its open structure (in line with Polanyi's analysis) to what is beyond empirical observation" helps avoid "the rationalistic and deterministic fallacy." Torrance appeals to "a *regulative force*, and indeed a *controlling source of information*" beyond the sheer organic structure and genetic components of the embryo, which again follows a biblical unitary view of body-soul and affirms "the human embryo as already a *human life*.[88]

He underscores a social or interpersonal view of the unborn child because "it is in and through relation with the mother that the embryonic being of the child begins his or her personal existence, and that it is through loving personalising relation with the mother that the tiny personal being of the foetus is nourished, and its embryonic personal response to the mother is developed, evident, for example, in recognition of and reaction to the mother's voice." "Certainly," he continues his theological ethic about and against abortion, "it is God himself who is the Creative Source of all personal being and inter-personal relations – he is the personalising Person, who brings us into personal life and being through the inter-personal activity of a father and mother, which begins with our conception, develops in our pre-natal life, reaches fruition in birth and childhood, and blossoms with the inter-personal life and love of a human family," an interpersonal bonding that "must be regarded as *personal*."[89]

In sum, "we must think of the human person as transcendentally determined in his or her existence as soul and body, which not only constitutes him or her as a personal human being before God, but maintains him or her in relation to him as the ultimate Ground and Source of his or

---

87 Torrance, *The Christian Doctrine of Marriage* (Edinburgh: Handsel Press, 1992), 3-4.

88 *Unborn Child*, 8-11.

89 Ibid., 15-7.

her creaturely order.... The human embryo is fully *human being, personal being* in the sight and love of his or her Creator, and must be recognised, accepted, and cherished as such, not only by his or her mother and father, but by science and medicine."[90]

Torrance addresses in more popular form his basic view of abortion to pro-life Presbyterians in North Carolina, to whom he repeated one of his basic axioms for his theological ethic: "As such we are ultimately to be understood not from an independent center in ourselves, but only from above and beyond ourselves in a unique relation to God."[91] He appeals to the Virgin birth as a compelling theological argument against abortion:

> It belongs to the very heart of the Gospel that the Word of God who was the eternal Son of God, of one being with the Father, and through whom all things were made, chose in his love to become incarnate in Jesus Christ, was conceived through the Holy Spirit in the womb of the Virgin Mary, and became a true human being. It is surely to him who became a holy embryo in the Virgin's womb, and was born of her to be the Savior of the world, that we must go, in order as Christians to understand what the unborn child is as an embodied human soul, and as one loved by the Lord Jesus who came to be the Savior of the human race. The eternal Word of God become incarnate *was and is himself the metaplan*, the creative and regulative force in the birth of each human being, come among us as one of us to be Lord and Savior of the human race![92]

Torrance also wrote an essay on Anselm as a way of discussing and relating **telling and doing the truth**. Here we see his integration of the epistemological with the ethical: knowing things *kata physin* ("in accordance with their nature"), which also means knowing God according to his nature and acting in accord with it. He notes the close relation "between telling the truth and doing the truth ... signifying, by word or act, that that which is, is what it is and what according to its nature it ought to be." Truth, then, refers "to a condition of reality beyond itself ... the truth or rightness of that to which it refers," from which "there derives a universal obligation for things to be true ... for truth is a demanded form of rightness: a thing is true not

---

90 Ibid., 18-9.

91 Torrance, *The Being and Nature of the Unborn Child* (Lenior, NC: Glen Lorien Books, 2000), 11.

92 Ibid., 13-4.

only when it is what it is but when it is rightly what according to its nature it ought to be."[93]

He agrees and insists with Anselm "that ethical acts and judgments are grounded in the ultimate Rightness and have to be understood in terms of the debt that it exacts," which pertains both to doing the truth and to telling the truth. So for Anselm and Torrance, "the truth of genuinely moral action is simply the rightness of will fulfilled for its own sake." Moral action is both rational and voluntary, "for only when the mind and will act together can the rightness of will be fulfilled for its own sake." In short, "[T]he rightness of sanctification depends on the rightness of its *end* and its *object*, of its *why* and its *what*, which are determined for it by an objective correctness . . ." and through which we participate "in the Supreme Truth or Supreme Rightness of God."[94]

Torrance, as a final example, wrote an entire monograph on **Law**, which continues to display a consistent theological social ethic that his critics simply ignore. He criticizes "modern ethics where the norms of behaviour are tracked back to mere convention and social utility, without any claim that they are objectively grounded in being or constrained by an order in the rational nature of things independent of ourselves" – e.g., the lack of a "deeper and more enduring foundation that we have allowed in our legal science or in our political constitution. We need to rediscover the ontology of juridical law," rather than a legal positivism that practices "the ontological uprooting of moral and judicial law from its objective ground in the Ultimate Truth and Rightness of God himself." Modern legal theory too often relies upon "a moral positivism, as ethical principles and concepts uprooted from their ontological grounds tend to be treated as little more than traditional arrangements deriving from the evolution of human relations or to be regarded merely as convenient social conventions which can have no more than an oblique relation to an objective basis if such an idea is to be entertained at all" – unlike modern physical science which "has moved from a positivist to a realist outlook . . ."[95]

Similar to his essay on Anselm and ethics, he argues that legal science must *think and behave* "strictly in accordance with the nature of things."

---

93 Torrance, "The Ethical Implications of Anselm's *De Veritate*," *Theologische Zeitschrift* 24 (1968), 309-11.

94 Ibid., 314-9.

95 Torrance, *Juridical Law and Physical Law: Toward a Realist Foundation for Human Law* (Eugene, OR: Wipf and Stock, 1997), ix-x, 2.

Similar to his essays on abortion, he bases the true nature of law on "the ontological substructure of personal and social relations" or "person-constituting relations," such as the human family which is "governed by mutual sharing, love and concern." This "ontological structure of interpersonal human relations . . . points all human law-making beyond itself to a normative source and self-sufficient ground in Almighty God."[96]

Torrance thus argues for a concept of order in a way that shows the integral relationship of his Christian ethic with his entire view of theology and science:

> Hence, far from thinking of the saving acts of God in Jesus Christ as in any way an interruption of the order of creation, or some sort of violation of natural law, we must rather think of the Incarnation, Passion and Resurrection of Christ . . . as the chosen way in which God, the ultimate Source of all rational order, brings his transcendent mind and will to bear upon the disordered structures of our creaturely existence in space and time.[97]

For the Incarnation of the Word is:

> the creative order of redeeming love, and the kind of order that is unable to reveal to us its own deepest secret but can only point mutely and indefinitely beyond itself. Yet since this is an order that we may apprehend only as we allow our minds to yield to the compelling claims of reality, it is found to be an order burdened with a latent imperative which we dare not, rationally or morally, resist, the order of how things actually are which we may appreciate adequately only as we let our minds grope out for what things are meant to be and ought to be.[98]

Summary

To recapitulate, Torrance affirms a soteriological suspension of autonomous ethics superseded by the vicarious humanity of Christ, which sanctifies human morality as people be and become who they truly are in union with Christ. Far from invalidating our humanity, Christ's humanity heals the

---

96 Ibid., 28, 41-5, 53.

97 Torrance, *The Christian Frame of Mind: Reason, Order, and Openness in Theology and Natural Science* (Colorado Springs, CO: Helmers & Howard, 1989), 21.

98 Ibid., 34.

ontological depths of our being to reorient and validate our human lives and actions in him. Torrance roots a Christian "moral ontology" in the very relational being of God himself, which suggests a filial, not a legal or moral, ethic. The critics of Torrance have failed to understand his unitary Christian theological ethic, based on a trinitarian-incarnational paradigm that addresses concrete personal and social issues. We have seen how the incarnate, crucified, and risen Christ upholds those on the margins of life, for example, women in ministry and the unborn child, affirming and redeeming the created order on behalf of those whose voices have been muted and marginalized. For Torrance, the very being and heart of God affirms, upholds, and sanctifies all of human life. Whether or not one agrees with his specific stances on such social issues, Torrance has articulated a thoroughly theological ethic of reconciliation in Christ, who effects the transformation of humanity and all personal and social structures on the basis of God's grace.

Chapter 2

Incarnational Social Ethics

If there are two sides to humanity," Ray Anderson proclaims, "Christ will be found on the wrong side."[1] Jesus embodied the unreserved presence of God with and for sinners. "Those who are well have no need of physician," Jesus declares, "but those who are sick. Go and learn what this means, 'I desire mercy, and not sacrifice.' For I came not to call the righteous, but sinners" (Mt. 9:12f.). Christ's incarnate humanity — his entire life, death, and resurrection among and on behalf of sinners — provides the basis for and the reality of reconciliation. He stands in our place and acts on our behalf to heal our humanity. His vicarious humanity — i.e., his substitutionary life and death in our place and representative humanity on our behalf — reconciles us to one another and to God. Social reconciliation is both an indicative and an imperative of the gospel of Jesus Christ, both gift and task, both command and promise.

An incarnational ethic is a filial ethic. As T. F. Torrance writes in his Introduction to *Jesus and the Christian*, by William Manson (his professor, colleague, and friend), and I will quote at length:

> If there is one theme more than another that runs throughout the essays collected in this volume it is the immediacy and realism with which the Kingdom of God apprehended by Jesus and actualized by Him through his life, death and resurrection, bears upon our daily life. In Jesus Himself the absolute of God has reached us in a context of grace and power. It is in grace that the Christian revelation begins and it is on grace that it rests — hence the whole of the Sermon on the Mount Manson claimed, must be interpreted in this light. But it is also in power that God's grace has broken into our midst, setting our life on a wholly new basis.... Christianity means a life in which we expose our whole existence to the drastic operation of God's living Word to us in Christ, which will not allow us to relax the eschatological tension

---

[1] Ray S. Anderson, *Historical Transcendence and the Reality of God* (Grand Rapids: Eerdmans, 1975), 252.

of the soul or take our eyes off the Ultimate Goal that lies ahead; a life in which we are summoned to bear the reproach of Christ in the world-mission of His Gospel, which is the true Christian approach to the altar; but it also means a life in which we are taken up in Jesus, through His incarnate fellowship with us in our weakness and His self-oblation through the Eternal Spirit to the Father, to participate in the transcendent worship of the heavenly Sanctuary. From beginning to end the Christian life is to be consecrated together with Christ in his self-consecration to God for our sakes and in Him to realize on earth the filial obedience of children to their heavenly Father.[2]

Christ's Incarnation as God's Identification with Sinners

Jesus does not simply sojourn among us, declares Athanasius, but also heals as a physician who touches our existence with his own being.[3] He bears, not merely cures, our sins (Mt. 8:17, Is. 53:4, 1 Pt. 2:24). "Christ does not heal us by standing over against us," writes James Torrance, for he heals our humanity in solidarity with us, as the sanctifying presence of God. "He is," Torrance continues, "the True Priest, bone of our bone, flesh of our flesh, who bears upon his divine heart our sins and injustices and who effects in his vicarious humanity our reconciliation."[4]

If the divine power of heaven had preserved its dignity by not coming into contact with diseased humanity on earth, then our sickness would not have received its cure and we would not have been healed. But God assumed human life from birth unto death, asserts Gregory of Nyssa, healing "all that lies between."[5] "For that which he has not assumed he has not healed," writes Gregory of Nazianzus in opposition to Apollinarianism, "but that which is united to his Godhead is also saved."[6]

---

2 Thomas F. Torrance, "Introduction" to William Manson, *Jesus and the Christian* (Grand Rapids: Eerdmans, 1967), 14.

3 Athanasius, "On the Incarnation of the Word," in *Christology of the Later Fathers*, ed. Edward R. Hardy (Philadelphia: Fortress, 1949), 97f.

4 James B. Torrance, "The Vicarious Humanity of Jesus Christ," in *The Incarnation: Ecumenical Studies in the Nicene-Constantinopolitan Creed, A.D. 38*, ed. Thomas F. Torrance (Edinburgh: Handsel Press, 1981), 130.

5 Gregory of Nyssa, "An Address on Religious Instruction," in *Christology*, ed., Hardy, 304f.

6 Gregory of Nazianzus, "Letters on the Apollinarian Controversy," in *Christology*, ed. Hardy, 218.

God in Christ assumed humanity in its wholeness to heal and sanctify our broken existence.[7]

He freely acted as the powerful one who assumed the form of weakness, the eternal one who revealed himself in space and time, and the Lord who came to us as a servant. The exaltation of Christ (Phil. 2:9ff.) is not in spite of, but because of, his humiliation (Phil. 2:6ff.). Paul's exhortation to unity (which precedes the kenotic hymn) should and may be obeyed because the Philippians have the mind of Christ, whose humility was grounded in the being of God.[8] Because God revealed who he is in Christ, we therefore ought to be who we are and are becoming in Christ, not merely by emulating his example but by participating in the vicarious obedience of the incarnate, crucified, and risen Christ.

Christ lived and died as the one on behalf of the many. The Old Testament concept of the one and the many implied a "corporate personality": one who acted on behalf of others both in a Godward and in a humanward movement.[9] Adam was the one who summed up the history of old humanity; Christ was the one who embodied the reality of new humanity.[10] Christ assumed and sanctified Jewish flesh, the one Israelite on behalf of the many, which served as "a mirror held up" to the faces "of all peoples."[11] He redeemed our unfaithful and disobedient humanity in and through his own humanity. The enfleshment of the Word, writes Irenaeus, summarized "the long history of the human race" to save and reconstitute humanity.[12] Christ assumed our flesh, not some foreign substance, and therefore recapitulated in himself "that original handiwork of the Father," which was lost in Adam yet restored in Christ. Our human flesh, being "nourished with the Body and Blood of the Lord" partakes of life in anticipation of the resurrection, "just as the bread which comes from the

---

7 Ibid., 219f.

8 Karl Barth, *Church Dogmatics*, IV/ 1, ed. Geoffrey W. Bromiley & Thomas F. Torrance, trans. Geoffrey W. Bromiley (Edinburgh: T & T Clark, 1956), 187ff., 193.

9 Aubrey R. Johnson, *The One and the Many in the Israelite Conception of God*, 2nd ed. (Cardiff: Univ. of Wales, 1961), 33f.

10 H. Wheeler Robinson, *Corporate Personality in Ancient Israel*, rev. ed. (Phila.: Fortress, 1980), 37; Jean de Fraine, *Adam and the Family of Man*, trans. D. Raible (Staten Island: Alba House, 1965), pp. 274f.

11 Barth, *Church Dogmatics*, IV/1, 171f.

12 Irenaeus, "Against Heresies," in *The Christological Controversy*, trans. & ed. Richard A. Norris (Phila.: Fortress, 1980), 49.

earth, having received the invocation of God, is no longer ordinary bread, but the Eucharist . . ."[13]

Christ is the truth about both God and humanity. He has satisfied in his humanity what God intended for us. He has realized both God's promise — "I will be your God" — and God's command — "and you shall be my people." He is, asserts Barth, both "the promise and the command, the Gospel and the Law, the address of God to man and the claim of God upon man."[14] In him, the command is also a promise, because God in Christ fulfills what he commands, hears what he speaks, and accomplishes what he wills.[15]

"The intra-trinitarian relations opened up to humanity," Alan Torrance declares, "through the incarnation of the Son as Jesus Christ underpin the entire witness and message of the New Testatament." He continues, ". . . we need to appreciate the two-fold movement represented in and through the hypostatic union, namely, that God comes to humanity *as God* (anhypostatic movement) and God comes to humanity *as man* and presents humanity redeemed and sanctified in himself to the Father (the enhypostatic, human-Godward movement)." Torrance is worth quoting at length:

> In Jesus Christ each and every one of us finds our worship, prayers, and intercessions lifted up, sanctified and presented by the one who is the sole Priest and Representative of each of us. The very nature of our ongoing life of worship and, indeed, ethics (worth-ship) is to be conceived, therefore, in terms of this very concrete participation, by the Spirit, in our sole priest, intercessor and *leitourgos*. In worship we are not 'turned back upon ourselves' to try and generate what God requires of us. Worship and, indeed, every facet of our response (all that is required of us by the *torah*) is to be conceived as participation, by grace, in Christ's fulfillment of these *dikaiomata*, in his Amen, in his 'Yes' to the Faither, and in his worship. In the Eucharist and in prayer and, indeed, in every facet of the Christian life the Spirit seeks to lift us up to share in his perfect response and ongoing worship offered on our behalf.[16]

---

13 Irenaeus, *The Scandal of the Incarnation: Irenaeus Against the Heresies*, ed. Hans Urs von Balthasar (San Fran.: Ignatius, 1981), 58-9, 92-3.

14 Barth, *Church Dogmatics*, IV/1, 53.

15 Ibid., 47.

16 Alan J. Torrance, "Introduction," *Trinity and Transformation: J. B. Torrance's Vision of Worship, Mission, and Society*, ed. Todd H. Speidell (Eugene, OR: Wipf & Stock, 2016), 10-11.

Douglas Campbell argues "that feedom denotes an aspect of the perfect obedience offered by Jesus's human to the divine will." Humans, therefore, find their true freedom in his perfect obedience for us — which means neither "an erasure of human activity by a divine covenant" nor "a dangerous excess of human freedom!" On the contrary, he insists (in agreement with J. B. Torrance) "that covenantal relationships come with unconditional expectations of behavior (covenantal ones)!" In fact, "ethical activity generated by the pressure of a loving covenantal relationship places the strongest pressures on an actor, as well as the most appropriate," pressures which create a reciprocity of unconditional love in social relationships.[17]

> Gospel and law are neither confused nor separated but fulfilled in Christ. He is the content of the gospel and the fulfillment of the law. God for us is the basis of what God wants with us and from us.[18] God's commands are weakened when they become the demands of a human "ought," or a contractual "if," for the law is weakened by the flesh. Yet what the law could not do on its own, God did for us in Christ (Rom. 8:3).[19] His vicarious obedience for us has fulfilled (but not abrogated) the law; hence, we shall (both as command and promise) acknowledge, love, and obey God in gratitude.[20]

James Torrance contrasts covenant and contract. He notes that a contract

> *is a legal relationship in which two people or two parties bind themselves together on mutual conditions* to effect some future result. The business world and poltical world are full of such contracts. They take the form 'If you do this, then I will do

---

17 Douglas A. Campbell, "Covenant or Contract in the Interpretation of Paul," ibid., 199-201. For a defense of a christocentric vs. anthropocentric understanding of the *pistis christou* debate (i.e., "the faith[fulness] *of* Christ" as a subjective genitive vs. "faith *in* Christ" as an objective genitive), see Douglas Campbell, "The Faithfulness of of Jesus Christ in Romans 3:22," in *The Faith of Jesus Christ: Exegetical, Biblical, and Theological Studies* ed. M. F. Bird & P. M. Sprinkle (Peabody, MA: Hendrickson, 2009), 57-72. Campbell's *magnum opus* is *The Deliverance of God: An Apocalyptic Rereading of Justification in Paul* (Grand Rapids: Eerdmans, 2009). For responses to Campbell, see *Beyond Old and New Perspectives on Paul: Reflections on the Work of Douglas Campbell*, ed. Chris Tilling (Eugene, OR: Cascade, 2014).

18 Karl Barth, *Community, State, and Church* (Gloucester, MA: Peter Smith, 1968), 76ff.

19 Ibid., 87.

20 Ibid., 81f.

that.' Society at large is built on a network of such contractual arrangements.

"There is no such thing as conditional love in God," he declares, for the "covenant of love" is *unconditioned* by us, for God's grace is "free grace" and *unconditionally* summons us to love of God and neighbor because God's grace is "costly grace."[21]

Our participation in the ministry of the incarnate one, who lived his life concretely in a particular place for others, lays a priority on localized love: first to family, then to neighbors and friends, and finally to "distant neighbors."[22] Christians in the U.S. must address race relations in their local churches before denouncing larger and more distant issues of systemic racism. They should engage in local forms of service before global (and often abstract) discussions of justice and equality. When they do respond to the global dimensions of Christian social responsibility, they will then do so with integrity; they will do so with a sense of the humanity of their (even distant) neighbor.

God thus binds humans to himself and to one another in the vicarious humanity of Christ, the one on behalf of the many. The incarnation testifies to God's identifying presence with us, healing what he assumes. The cross presupposes the incarnation as God's solidarity with sinners, and the incarnation leads to the cross, for God identifies with sinners from birth unto death to sanctify the whole of our humanity.

By way of transition, Markus Barth warns against a Platonizing "incarnational principle," which is "magnified at the expense of the crucifixion." Otherwise, Jesus is merely "a noble figure, who pursues his noble goals to the bitter end." But this is a tragic end that leads to no better than a Platonic immortality of the soul, "which attempts to bypass or to sweeten the bitterness of death's taste." "If, however, Christ's death is a sacrifice," he concludes,

> then the death of the true man, Jesus Christ, and the limitation of every man's life in time, are not tragic features which disturb or interrrupt an otherwise wonderful process of continuous 'incarnational' influx of the divine into the material. Rather, it is revealed by the true man that all humanity must and can stand

---

21 James B. Torrance, "The Unconditional Freedom of Grace" in *Trinity and Transformation*, 280-82.

22 The phrase is Karl Barth's, *Church Dogmatics*, III/4, trans. A. T. Mackay et al. (1961), 285ff.

before God only in accepting the limits which God has set by creating time; in accepting the vocation to glorify God even in a most horrible death. Life in time is then not a process between the spiritual and material realms, but a glorious opportunity given by God to love God and one's fellow man 'to the end' (cp. John 13.1; 19.30).[23]

Christ's Crucifixion as God's Confrontation with Sinners

Christ's death on the cross "reveals the full seriousness of the human situation."[24] Human nature is radically sinful from the center of its being throughout the whole of its existence.[25] No "attractive realism" or "Christian humanitarianism" will do, for God's grace overthrows all human attempts to establish the kingdom of God on earth (cf. Lk. 4:5ff.).[26] Christ identifies with humans, then, to confront them with God's grace for sinners.

The crucified Christ continues God's solidarity with estranged and lost humanity to effect the *reality* of reconciliation, which should be distinguished from a contemporary Anabaptist view of the cross. For example, Jesus' baptism is the inauguration, declares John Howard Yoder, and his cross the culmination of God's kingdom, which creates "a new possibility of human, social, and therefore political relationships" — that is, "a new kind of community leading a radically new kind of life."[27] Only at one point, asserts Yoder, is Jesus "consistently" and "universally" our example: at the cross.[28] Jesus' "motto of revolutionary subordination" and "social style" of "new community" reject violence, for Christ's submission to the cross is "the model of Christian social efficacy."[29]

"Jesus' story is a social ethic," Stanley Hauerwas suggests in line with Yoder, and "people who are willing to take his cross as their story

---

23 Markus Barth, *"Was Christ's Death A Sacrifice?"* (Edinburgh: Oliver and Boyd, SJOT Occasional Papers No. 9, 1961), 52. Of related interest, see Oscar Cullmann, *Immortality of the Soul or Resurrection of the Dead?: The Witness of the New Testament* (Eugene, OR: Wipf and Stock, 1964).

24 Barth, *Church Dogmatics*, IV/ 1, 219.

25 Ibid., 492.

26 Ibid., 262.

27 John Howard Yoder, *The Politics of Jesus* (Grand Rapids: Eerdmans, 1972), 63.

28 Ibid., 97, 134.

29 Ibid., 190, 250.

... become the continuation of that ethic in the world."[30] The church, he continues, exemplifies the ethic of Jesus as a "contrast model" to the world, tells the story of Jesus, and continues the truth of God's kingdom.[31] The cross in Anabaptist thought is "a way of life to be lived among people" based on the "principle" of "the way of the cross."[32] The church, then, applies this "kingdom idea" to practical life in the context of a Christ/world dualism by being an alternative community.[33]

The crucified humanity of Christ, however, should not be treated as a possibility of our radical discipleship; rather, it effects the reality of reconciliation in humanity. "And a cross without its humanity," Anderson writes, "is a cross without its power of reconciliation.... But the truth of the Gospel is not that humanity has been put on the cross; it is rather that the cross has been sunk deep into humanity."[34] "The clue, therefore, to social justice," he asserts, "is not the justice of God as an abstract principle but his humanity as an historical and continuing power of reconciliation."[35] The crucified Christ stands in solidarity with humanity, not merely as an example of confrontation with the world to be imitated by us but as the reality of new humanity in which we must and may participate.

Christ gives us himself, not merely a radical ethic of confrontational discipleship. He confronts us with his true humanity and our restored humanity, not simply slogans of peace and justice nor pronouncements against social sins that characterize a politicized church, which seems

---

30 Stanley Hauerwas, *A Community of Character* (Notre Dame: Univ. of Notre Dame, 1981), 40, 44.

31 Ibid., 50ff. Hauerwas does recall a significant realization in 1986 in a conversation with Barth scholar Nigel Biggar. He recounts this significant occasion: "... Nigel observed, rather astutely, that for all my insistence that Christian ethics be Christian, in spite of my repeated and tiresome emphasis on the unavoidable reality of the church for how we think about the nature of the moral life, God was nonetheless curiously missing from my work." Stanley Hauerwas, "The Truth about God: The Decalogue as Condition for Truthful Speech," in Alan J. Torrance and Michael Banner, eds., *The Doctrine of God and Theological Ethics* (London: T & T Clark, 2006), 85.

32 Guy F. Hersberger, *The Way of the Cross in Human Relations* (Scottdale, PA: Herald, 1958), 33, 43.

33 Robert Friedmann, *The Theology of Anabaptism* (Scottdale, PA: Herald, 1973), 41, 43.

34 Ray S. Anderson, "The Little Man on the Cross," *Reformed Journal* (Nov. 1982):16; later published in *The Shape of Practical Theology: Empowering Ministry with Theological Praxis* (Downers Grove, IL: IVP, 2001), 312-16.

35 Ibid., 15.

not to need Christ as it announces its own agenda. Christ and his work, however, stand "against us" precisely because he is "for us."[36] He substitutes his life and death in our place, representing us to God in his whole atoning life and death.[37] The vicarious work of Christ as "the Judge judged in our place," declares Barth, effects atonement for us; otherwise, "everything else will be left hanging in the void as an anthropological or psychological or sociological myth, and sooner or later it will break and fall to the ground."[38]

The atonement originates in the Fatherhood of God and the Sonship of Christ, John McLeod Campbell argues, and results in our life of sonship and daughterhood.[39] Our proper response to Christ's atoning work, he continues, is filial "trust in a Father's heart," not "trust in the judicial grounds" of a legal title. Our "filial confidence," rather than "legal confidence," indicates a response of sonship and daughterhood to the heart of God revealed in Christ.[40]

Evangelical repentance posits God as Father and humans as brothers and sisters, based on the Godward and humanward aspects of the atonement. Christ offered his life on our behalf to heal our estranged and hostile humanity; in him, we know God as Father and others as brothers and sisters.[41] There is one grace of the gospel. Christ is both the Son of the Father and the Brother of humanity; our relations toward God and one another are healed in the crucified Christ.

The 1984 movie *Places in the Heart* portrays a young black boy who accidentally kills a white sheriff. The townspeople, in turn, brutally and shamelessly kill the boy. A black man passes through town looking for work. He and the sheriff's widow provide mutual help for each other, the man needing work to survive and the widow needing help with her crops to save her property from foreclosure. In the end, the local church celebrates the sacrament of communion: the townspeople, the white sheriff's widow, the black man — even the white sheriff and the black boy — are all present, passing the bread and the cup to one another.

---

36 Barth, *Church Dogmatics*, IV/1, 256f.

37 Ibid., 259.

38 Barth, *Church Dogmatics*, IV/3, 273.

39 John McLeod Campbell, *The Nature of the Atonement* (London: Macmillan, 1878), 295.

40 Ibid., 299.

41 Ibid., 315f.

INCARNATIONAL SOCIAL ETHICS

Christ has made us fellow citizens, no longer outsiders vs. insiders. He has created peace between us, not merely peace of mind. He has abolished our enmity and restored our humanity in himself, the true human. Christ "has broken down the dividing wall of hostility," declares the author of Ephesians, and has created in himself one new humanity "through the cross" (Eph. 2:14ff.). The crucifixion of the Jewish, circumcised, male Jesus of Nazareth, Anderson proclaims, ends racial, religious, and sexual prerogatives. Jesus brought his Jewish, circumcised, and male flesh to the cross and thereby abolished these criteria of inclusion.[42] Jesus Christ is the new criterion for social relationships between men and women, Jew and Gentile, black and white.

"*He is in person the peace between us*," comments Markus Barth on Eph. 2:14, or literally: "He is our peace." "*He has broken down the dividing wall*" (between Gentiles and Jews) or literally: "the division-wall of the fence." "The Greek noun *mesotoichon*, translated by the adjective 'dividing,' he notes,

> is not found in pre-Christian Greek, and nowhere in the NT except here. It means a partition inside a house. The other term, *phragmos*, translated by 'wall,' signifies originally a fence or railing erected for protection rather than separation. The combination of the two Greek nouns yields a composite sense: it is a wall that prevents certain persons from entering a house or a city (cf. 2:19), and is as such a mark of hostility (2:14, 16), as, e.g. a ghetto wall, the Iron Curtain, the Berlin Wall, a racial barrier, or a railroad track that separates the right from the wrong side of the city, not to speak of the wall between state and church.[43]

"To confess Jesus Christ," Markus Barth continues, "is to affirm the abolition and end of division and hostility, the end of separation and segregation, the end of enmity and contempt, and the end of every sort of ghetto!" When one says "Christ," he or she says "reconciliation" or "peace," which means the "'abolition' and 'abrogation' of every and and all hostility (2:14f.)." He concludes and proclaims,

> Abolition and peace — these great words will keep us from dreaming of, or scoffing at, a sexless, raceless, homeless, neuter

---

42 Ray S. Anderson, "The Resurrection of Jesus as Hermeneutical Criterion" (Part I), *TSF Bulletin* 9 (Jan/Feb. 1986): 10.

43 See his two-volume commentary on Ephesians: *Ephesians 1-3* and *Ephesians 4-6* (Garden City, NY: Double Day, 1974), especially Vol. 1, 262-64.

> superman, whom Christianity allegedly ought to promote or to produce. The words 'neither Jew nor Greek, neither slave nor free man, neither male nor female; you are all one in Christ Jesus (Gal. 3:28; Col. 3:11; I Cor. 12:13) by which Paul describes Christ's work, do by no means wipe out or deny distinctions between nations, sexes, classes, and occupations. Otherwise Paul would not have included in his letters special exhortations for Jews and Greeks (Rom. 2:17ff.; 11:13ff.), husbands and wives (Eph. 2; 5:22ff.; Col. 3:18ff.), slaves and masters (Eph. 6:5 ff.), etc. But, faith in Christ, even Christ himself, means that the two — whatever their distinctions are — can and do live together: those who were formerly opposed, mutually exclusive, separated by what seemed to be an unsurmountable wall. To say 'Christ' means to say community, co-existence, a new life, peace (2:14).[44]

"When his peace," Barth concludes, "is deprived of its social, national, or economic dimensions, when it is distorted or emasculated so much that only 'peace of mind' enjoyed by saintly individuals is left — then Jesus Christ is being flatly denied."[45]

The eschatological freedom of being in Christ, in whom there is neither male nor female (Gal. 3:28), Leonhard Goppelt argues, does not obliterate our humanity, for there is also an eschatological tension of living within one's present state (1 Cor. 7:20).[46] We are male and female in Christ, and therefore one, and yet we are still male and female. Christ radically qualifies our maleness and femaleness, breaking down hostilities, prerogatives, and self-assertion, and liberating humans to be reconciled as males and females.

Our concrete humanity cannot be simply set aside, such as Letty Russell's assertion that we should explore "experimental life-styles that seek to overcome old dichotomies that we have inherited: clergy/laity, male/female, rich/poor, black/white, gay/straight"; she lists several "alternatives" and "new forms of human sexuality," such as "communal marriages, serial mating, single parent arrangements, cluster families, polygamy, homosexual arrangements."[47] Her abstract understanding of "partnership," however,

---

44 Markus Barth, *The Broken Wall: A Study of the Epistle of the Ephesians* (Phila.: Judson, 1959), 43-4. Also see his *The People of God* (Sheffield, Eng.: SJOT, 1983).

45 Barth, *The Broken Wall*, 45.

46 Leonhard Goppelt, *Theology of the New Testament*, 2, trans. John Alsup, ed. Jürgen Roloff (Grand Rapids: Eerdmans, 1982), 146, 157.

47 Letty M. Russell, *The Future of Partnership* (Phila.: Westminster, 1979), 132, and *Human Liberation in a Feminist Perspective — A Theology* (Philadelphia: Westminster, 1974), 151f.

undermines our ontological differentiation as male and female and reduces sexuality merely to biological differentiation. Christ, the Creator and Redeemer, holds out his true humanity to us, so that we may be who we are in him precisely as male and female. Christ's humanity, not traditionalist or feminist formulations of what it means to be male and female, affirms, qualifies, and liberates us as men and women in relationship to one another.

The crucified Christ is the "end" of humanity in a double sense: the discontinuity of sinful criteria ("end" as terminus) and the continuity of created humanity ("end" as telos, based on the eschaton of Christ's true humanity). The crucified Christ confronts hostility, discrimination, oppression, and exclusion; he imparts his true and new humanity as the basis for and the reality of social reconciliation.

Christ's Resurrection as God's Re-formation of Sinners

Christ's double movement of humiliation and exaltation, suggests Barth, portrays the Son of God going into the far country and the Son of Man returning home, bringing along the humanity he assumed to present it to the Father and give it new life.[48] The resurrection, argues T. F. Torrance, unveils the cross as "the recreation and final affirmation" of humanity.[49] The resurrection, he continues, demonstrates to us "the *wholeness* of our redemption in a *whole* Christ," and hence concludes our adoption through Christ as his fellow sons and daughters of the Father.[50] The crucified Christ destroys the disobedience of old humanity, Barth believes, and the risen Christ fulfills the obedience of new humanity.[51]

"The risen Christ," Jürgen Moltmann importantly reminds us, "is and remains the crucified Christ."[52] A social ethic based merely on the resurrection would degenerate into enthusiasm. "The radical solution," Bonhoeffer warns, sees only the ultimate and ignores the penultimate. One is either "for Christ" or "against him." Whether withdrawing from the

---

48 Barth, *Church Dogmatics*, IV/2, 100.

49 Thomas F. Torrance, *Space, Time and Resurrection* (Grand Rapids: Eerdmans, 1976), 56, 58.

50 Ibid., 66, 69.

51 Karl Barth, *Church Dogmatics*, II/1, ed. G. W. Bromiley & T. F. Torrance, trans. T. H. L. Parker et al. (Edinburgh: T & T Clark, 1957), 626.

52 Jürgen Moltmann, *Theology of Hope*, trans. James W. Leitch (NY: Harper & Row, 1967), 171.

world or improving the world, the radical hates the world as it is. "The radical cannot forgive God His creation."[53] The compromise solution, on the other hand, sets apart "the last Word ... from all preceding words," so that the penultimate is not threatened by the ultimate.[54] The compromiser hates the ultimate and excludes it from penultimate matters. "The Christian spirit of compromise," he declares, "arises from hatred of the justification of the sinner by grace alone."[55] "Radicalism hates the real," he summarizes, "and compromise hates the word."[56]

The penultimate precedes the ultimate and yet is only validly determined by the ultimate. "Method," Bonhoeffer charges, "is a way from the penultimate to the ultimate. Preparation of the way is a way from the ultimate to the penultimate," for Christ himself prepares the way.[57] Feeding the hungry should not serve as a technique for preaching the gospel, for example, for proclaiming the incarnate one binds us in solidarity with the hungry, the homeless, the naked, the sick, and the imprisoned. Both the ultimate and the penultimate have "seriousness and validity" and a closely allied task, which is "to fortify the penultimate with a more emphatic proclamation of the ultimate, and also to protect the ultimate by taking due care for the penultimate."[58]

"The *pro-missio* of the kingdom," Moltmann agrees, "is the ground of the mission of love to the world."[59] The mission before the mission, the gracious work of God in Christ, leads the church in service. God's ultimate word of justification orients and prepares the way for penultimate acts of service and mission. But the "eschatological proviso" of the resurrection is the crucified Christ, not an *eschatologia gloriae*.[60] The crucified God provides hope as a realistic foundation for social transformation in the midst of present contradictions and in the expectation of the promised future.[61]

---

53 Dietrich Bonhoeffer, *Ethics*, ed. Eberhard Bethge (NY: Macmillan, 1955), 129.
54 Ibid., 127.
55 Ibid., 129f.
56 Ibid., 130.
57 Ibid., 141.
58 Ibid., 142.
59 Moltmann, *Hope*, 224.
60 Ibid., 159f.
61 Ibid., 84, 86.

Barth and T. F. Torrance criticize, however, the eschatological emptiness of an abstract concept of "hope."[62] The community of the incarnate, crucified, and risen Christ lives as the continued presence of Christ himself, whose Spirit leads and empowers the church's mission between Christ's ascension and advent. Christ's Spirit enables the church to participate in the risen Christ's service to the Father, who sends the church into the world.

Torrance announces,

> That God the transcendent Creator of the universe and the infinite Source of all its structure and order should thus become one of us and one with is in the birth, life, passion and resurrection of Jesus Christ in such a way as to effect a renewing of the creation and the setting of it on a new basis in which it is eternally bound up with the life of God himself, makes our minds reel with its immeasurable significance; but what is particularly staggering is the fact that it gives Jesus Christ a place of cosmic significance, making him, man of earth as he the incarnate Son of God is, the point of supreme focus for the whole universe of space and time, by reference to which all its meaning and destiny are finally to be discerned.[63]

"The resurrection of Jesus Christ," he concludes, "and of human nature in him is therefore the foundation and source of a profound and radically new humanism."[64]

Markus Barth, commenting again on Ephesians, notes that the resurrection of Christ is 1. an act by the *mighty* and *gracious* action of God alone; 2. an act of *cosmic* significance, including nature and history, society and the psyche, and "all principalities and powers," none of which "appears to be so omnipotent, final, and devestating as death," over which the risen Jesus triumps; and 3. a *final* act of confirmation: "Therefore, we need not vaguely wish or dream that there might be sometime, somewhere, somehow,

---

62 Karl Barth, *Letters*, 1961-1968, ed. Jürgen Fangmeier & Heinrich Stoevesandt, trans. & ed. G. W. Bromiley (Grand Rapids: Eerdmans, 1981), 175; Torrance, *Resurrection*, 25f. Also consider Moltmann's "trinitarian" theology of the cross, which neglects the role of the Spirit and, in the end, merely relies on psychoanalysis and socialism to provide a hermeneutic of psychological and political liberation, respectively. See Jürgen Moltmann, *The Crucified God*, trans. R. A. Wilson & J. Bowden (NY: Harper & Row, 1974), 243, 246; chs. 7, 8.

63 Torrance, *Resurrection*, 21f.

64 Ibid., 79.

hope... Rather, Ephesians asserts that there *is* hope and security and peace ... established by, before, and with God."⁶⁵ The risen One, he continues, "involves the lives of the many on earth": 1. as "a miracle which affects our being as radically and miraculously as it affected Him who was buried in the garden"; 2. as meaning "that with the supplication and intercession of Christ (Heb. 5:7f.; 7:25) and with the person of Jesus Christ himself, all our human affairs, our very predicament and condition, have been accepted by God, taken up, given hope, installed in a place of glory"; and 3. as implying that we have a "full share in what is human" based on Christ's exaltation from death and raising us to new life, truly and concretely, in, with, and through him.⁶⁶

Gary Deddo warns that the church should not simply proclaim "a *message* about Christ": "No, Christ came to give us a healed, restored and reconciled humanity. That was what he held out to us; his own humanity in right relationship to God and in right relationship to others." We therefore share with our neighbors the same humanity that Christ assumed and healed, Deddo concludes, and are now free to act towards our neighbors "on the basis of our shared true idenity forged and revealed in Jesus Christ, who as Lord and Savior offers us a share in his judged, healed, reconciled, and renewed all-inclusive humanity." To quote Deddo at length by way of summary:

> Who was Jesus Christ and what did he come to accomplish? He was the eternal Son of God, who out of his love and mercy assumed our humanity to make it his own, recreated it in himself, reconciled it to God in order to give us back a healed humanity in right relationship with God and others. Taking on a broken and alienated humanity, he has 'made both one' creating 'in himself one new humanity' (Eph. 2:14, 15). Salvation, as sharing in the Son's communion with the Father in the Spirit, meant God's purpose for humanity was brought to its *telos*, its final purpose in him, humanity fully alive, as Irenaeus had expressed it. In receiving the gift of sharing in the Son's communion with the Father we receive our healed, forgiven, and reconciled humanity. In receiving our human nature in Christ, we become fully human as God intended it from the beginning of creation.⁶⁷

---

65 *The Broken Wall*, 53-5.

66 Ibid., 56-9.

67 Gary Deddo, "James B. Torrance on The All-Inclusive Humanity of Christ," in *Trinity and Transformation*, 274-5.

Christian Ethics as *Participatio Christi*

Jesus Christ enacts God's love for his creation, his judgment upon sin, and his restoration of the fallen order. A Christian ethic based solely on the incarnation would lead to compromise, and based solely on the cross or resurrection it would lead to radicalism or enthusiasm. "In Jesus Christ," asserts Bonhoeffer, "we have faith in the incarnate, crucified and risen God." "There could be no greater error," he insists, "than to tear these three elements apart . . ."[68] The incarnate, crucified, and risen Christ has upheld God's covenant with humanity by identifying with us sinners, confronting our rebellious nature, and transforming who we are.

In Christ, God himself was present reconciling all things to himself (Col. 1:19f.). The vicarious humanity of Christ provides an objective reality of reconciliation over and against a subjective potentiality of self-justification. Christian ethics must not become an autonomous or independent subject separate from theology, for in his humanity Christ both reveals God to us and reconciles us to God and one another. A Christian ethic, therefore, presupposes intrinsic ontological grounds for reconciliation in the humanity of Christ, rather than the abstract and independent nature of a universal moral law or utilitarian calculus.

A Christian social ethic must attest to the concrete reality of our restored relationships in Christ. He does not merely leave his life and teaching for us to copy and embody in this world — as if we, rather than his Spirit, continue his presence and work in this world — but he continues to re-*present* himself as the ongoing reality of social reconciliation and true humanity. We do not need to become poor, pacifist, and powerless *like him* — unless Christ freely chooses to lead us into this lifestyle. Rather, we must be who we are — such as poor or rich, black or white, male or female — and are becoming *in him*.

Christ presents himself in the depths of human need — the hungry, the thirsty, the naked, the sick, the imprisoned (Mt. 25:31ff.). The stranger among us, the homeless and psychologically debilitated, may be the place of Christ's presence among us. The Gospel of Matthew does not exhort us simply to be like Christ — ministering to the needy "as Jesus would," which implies that he is not actively present but merely serves as a model for our social action. Matthew proclaims that Christ discloses himself through the stranger, so that we must be where Christ is and act where he acts,

---

68 Bonhoeffer, *Ethics*, 130f.

participating by the Spirit in Christ's ongoing ministry and mission in the world. By meeting the stranger, by entering into a distinctively human relationship with those to whom the government may or may not dispense its services and programs, we will meet Christ himself and find our own humanity.

God in Christ, asserts Barth, "is not good for himself"; he "is really good for us." For he "does not stand on that pretended frontier," Barth continues,

> where a smaller lack of goodness can regard itself as good in the face of a larger lack of goodness. He removes this frontier. He also removes the frontier that separates God's goodness from the lack of it which characterizes us all. He proclaims the forgiveness of sins. He opens the closed door of righteousness from within instead of rejoicing at being within and hiding himself behind the door. He brings the unrighteous in instead of talking to them through the closed door and taking pleasure in their being outside. . . . He thus spends his life, pours it out, and finally pours out his very blood for the hardened, the dejected and the hostile: not asking what he will get out of it; not asking anything, but simply acting for those who do not deserve it, turning to them as the Lamb of God which really takes away the sin of the world, which really takes it away (cf. John 1:29). This, then, is the divine goodness in the human goodness of Jesus of Nazareth: goodness which this man does not for a moment possess without giving it away.[69]

Christ gives his sanctified humanity to us, so that we may partake of him and his goodness. A Christian ethic must offer no abstract good, but should rather attest to the goodness of God revealed in Christ and given to us by the Spirit. The will of God, insists Bonhoeffer, is neither a mere idea, "still demanding to become real," nor what exists, which would simply require "submissive acquiescence," but a reality both in and against what exists.[70]

"The problem of Christian ethics," however, "is the realization among God's creatures of the revelational reality of God in Christ. . . ."[71] The Spirit of Christ both commands and enables us to participate in the revealing and reconciling work of God in Christ. Our participation in Christ's self-giving solidarity with the world attests to the primary reality that Jesus

---

69 Karl Barth, *Ethics*, ed. Dietrich Braun, trans. G. W. Bromiley (NY: Seabury, 1981), 339f.

70 Bonhoeffer, *Ethics*, 212.

71 Ibid., 190.

Incarnational Social Ethics

Christ gives his life for the world; hence, we serve as Christ's witnesses and servants in the world.

The love of neighbor, Barth argues, does not mean that we repeat or replace Christ's action of love, but that we witness to the reconciling action of God in Christ by meeting "our neighbors truly and honestly only as lost ourselves, i.e., exactly as we are, and not in the role of saviors." There is one Savior, he continues, who does not permit us to shield ourselves from our neighbor with our presumed goodness, but who commands us to "be fundamentally open to others," precisely as sinners to fellow-sinners.[72] God shows us our neighbors as brothers and sisters.

Christian life and neighborly love, Paul Molnar underscores, is a gift of God's grace. He writes,

> Just as we may know God himself in history only as we are known by him in the miraculous action of the Holy Spirit of Jesus Christ himself, and therefore only in union with Christ by grace and through faith, so we may live freely, that is, in and from the truth itself, as we live our reconciled lives and our new humanity in and from Christ alone, and therefore in faith and hope and thus also in love by loving God and our neighbors.[73]

God binds us together in filial relations in the vicarious humanity of our Brother Jesus Christ. Legal demands for social justice may provide rights, but not affirmation; legally assured conditions, but not personal relations; equality, but not respect; liberty, but not freedom. Affirmative action, for example, may be an expedient measure to correct societal injustices, but the gospel calls us beyond (even though including) rights to reconciliation and responsibility, because God has bound us to one another in Christ. We need each other as male and female, Jew and Gentile, slave and free, and to hear the gospel of Christ's reconciling work.

The basic form of humanity is social, reflecting the very image of the triune God. Christ offered his life among humans as a service to the Father and in the Spirit. He, as the one on behalf of the many, gave himself for the life of the world. He humanized our sinful and divisive social existence in his humanity, and enabled us to be who we are and are becoming in him.

Our cohumanity, our being in communion with others, requires human distinctives of social reconciliation. Cohumanity, Barth suggests,

---

72   Barth, *Ethics*, 343f.

73   Paul D. Molnar, *Faith, Freedom and the Spirit: The Economic Trinity in Barth, Torrance and Contemporary Theology* (Downers Grove: IVP, 2015), 374.

implies mutual seeing and being seen, so that we see each other eye-to-eye. To look the other in the eye and to let the other look into our own eye reveals the tendency to depersonalization: systematization in the social sciences (and theology!), the centralization of political economy, and the impersonalization of bureaucracy.[74]

Cohumanity also indicates a mutual speaking and hearing, so that we communicate mouth-to-ear. To speak as an expression of the self and to hear the other's self-expression manifests human communication, which addresses the other and is addressed by the other in a mutual penetration of personal being and knowing.[75] A human encounter of reciprocity does not allow talking past each other — "two monologues do not constitute dialogue"! — but with and to one another, for otherwise our words are "inhuman and barbaric," empty words which betray empty people.[76] The Jewish-Christian dialogue, for example, can neither permit one partner to discount in advance the other's position, which would force the other to surrender his or her "soul as a condition of dialogue,"[77] nor allow either partner to withhold judgment or evade the other's judgment.[78] Ecumenical and interfaith dialogue must include both genuine hearing and critique.

Cohumanity also affirms a mutual assistance and being assisted, so that we help each other hand-to-hand. To reach out my hand and to receive your hand expresses a concrete awareness of you as my fellow-human. We do not aid each other in the role of God, but only in a relative, though definite, way. Nor ought we to portray the unhealthy altruism that "helps" but does not stand by the other, for we must offer and receive the concrete solidarity of truly human help.[79]

Cohumanity, finally, suggests a mutual gladness of seeing and being seen, speaking and hearing, receiving and offering help, so that

---

74 Karl Barth, *Church Dogmatics*, III/2, ed. G. W. Bromiley & T. F. Torrance, trans. Harold Knight et al. (Edinburgh: T & T Clark, 1960), 250ff.

75 Ibid., 252ff.

76 Ibid., 259f.

77 Eugene B. Borowitz, *Contemporary Christologies: A Jewish Response* (NY: Paulist, 1980), 34.

78 Helmut Gollwitzer, *An Introduction to Protestant Theology*, trans. D. Cairn (Phila.: Westminster, 1982), 122.

79 Barth, *Church Dogmatics*, III/2, 260ff. Barth should lay more emphasis on the aspect of being helped, which he states but does not develop, for mutuality — being with the other — extends beyond charity — giving to the other.

we encounter one another heart-to-heart. To be glad means to live in correspondence with one's determination as a covenant-partner of God and one's fellow humanity. A neutral position in which one can choose between "gladly" and "reluctantly" indicates inhuman aloofness — "neutrally" is thus the real alternative to "gladly" — but true freedom gladly exists with the other."[80] Gladness with the other neither loses oneself in the other nor uses the other for oneself, but affirms the freedom to be oneself with the other and to be with the other in mutual openness, communion, and action.

The Elephant Man, a movie depicting the deformity of John Merrick and the inhumanity of society, limns the reality of human healing and reconciliation. The doctor who rescued the "Elephant Man" from the circus and displayed him as a medical abnormality eventually discovered that he was not an idiot but a human being. The doctor himself became transformed and discovered his own humanity. The woman who visited John Merrick treated him as a fellow human being — looking him in the eye, speaking with him, touching his hand, and enjoying his company. This human encounter healed him — not as a miraculous physical healing, but as a recovery of the humanity of which he had been robbed, which is perhaps the greater miracle. Despite the lack of physical healing, he died in peace.

Christ assumed our humanity to make us whole. He did not "merely help His fellows from without," Barth declares, "standing alongside, making a contribution and then withdrawing again and leaving them until further help is perhaps required." On the contrary, He gave "Himself to them" and made "their state and fate His own cause..."[81] He affirmed and transformed our humanity in his humanity as the very work of God himself.[82]

God assumed our humanity in Jesus of Nazareth, healed our humanity with his own being, and gave our sanctified humanity back to us. The Spirit of Christ commands and enables us to participate by grace in the vicarious humanity of Christ. We must, and may, live in the reconciled reality of our cohumanity in Christ by acknowledging the humanity of our neighbor. The incarnate Christ, who has assumed and healed our humanity, calls us to believe and repent in response to his reconciling work. The church cannot call the world to social repentance

---

80 Ibid., 265ff.
81 Ibid., 212.
82 Ibid., 220.

when it has not repented of its own social sins and its own agenda to improve the world. Instead of making endless pronouncements on the way the world ought to be, the church must first believe and practice the reality of social reconciliation.

The church does have a message to the world, which should be expressed in a renewed social practice. The church may issue a summons to the world to stand with it in evangelical social repentance; believing, confessing, and re-*present*-ing God's reconciling work in Christ. It cannot trivialize the impact of the gospel on human life by limiting its message to a list of social concerns and duplicating the role of a social agency. The church of the triune God, who is not a unitarian monad or solitary deity, must stand with and for those in need, that the church itself may continue to meet Christ in the midst of life (Mt. 25:31ff.).

James Torrance underscores that the gospel of grace in Christ calls us to "evangelical repentance," not "legal repentance." The latter reduces the gospel to the conditions of a contract or the moral mandates and self-based calls for social action and justice, which throw us back upon our own humanity. The former, however, "is our response to the word of the Cross which through the Spirit converts and heals and reconciles." "God's love," Torrance concludes, "so understood, should find focal expression at the Lord's table, for such love is creative of community, for there Christ gathers his people and gives himself to them freely and unconditionally by the Spirit and lifts us up out of ourselves and our introspectiveness and social lethargy" — freeing us to love God and all people in the name of Christ, converting "us into being a loving, caring, and believing community, members of his missionary body in the world."[83]

Christ, T. F. Torrance proclaims, frees us from being "the prisoner of an ethical or legal order" from which we cannot extricate ourselves and within which we cannot bridge the gap between ourselves and God. "But God in his free grace has come in Jesus Christ," he continues, to redeem humanity from this "helpless condition under the tyranny and curse of the law" and to lift us "up into living fellowship and loving communion with God the Father." "It was in his resurrection," Torrance concludes,

> that he broke through the nomistic form of our existence, rising again no longer in the form of a servant under the law, but in the

---

[83] Torrance, "Unconditional Freeness of Grace," 284-86. Also see Andrew Torrance, "John Calvin and James Torrance's Evangelical Vision of Repentance," also in *Trinity and Transformation*, 134-56.

form of the life-giving New Man, entirely and fully human, yet man no longer confined to the kind of limits that are imposed on us in our fallen world by the time-form of law or by the nomistic form of time. However, far from violating or abrogating time, he redeemed it. Just as in justification the law was not destroyed but established, so in the resurrection time is not annihilated but recreated, for it is taken up in Christ, sanctified in his human life and transformed in his resurrection as man.[84]

We participate, Torrance suggests, "in this new creation and its redeemed time . . . as the Body of Christ, the body not only of the crucified but of the risen Christ, the Body upon which he has poured out his Spirit as he ascended to fill all things, the Body which, though on earth and within history, is yet made participant in his risen power." "In other words," he summarizes,

> though risen with Christ and already a partaker through the Spirit in the new creation, the Church is sent like Christ into the world as the servant of the Lord, humbling itself and containing itself in *kenosis* within the limits and laws of this world in order to proclaim the Gospel of reconciliation and to live out reconciliation within conditions of fallen human existence.[85]

"What shall we do?" questioned those who heard Peter's sermon at Pentecost in response to the preaching of the gospel (Acts 2:37). "Repent, and be baptized," Peter replied, "every one of you in the name of Jesus Christ . . ." (Acts 2:38). A distinctively Christian ethic does not substitute social needs or moral mandates for the radical message of the gospel and the comprehensive claim of Christ on our lives. The church's proclamation of the gospel is not a mere matter of social concern, responsibility, and justice, but an evangelical summons to social repentance and renewal, which the church itself must first believe and practice. The church goes into the world to participate in the reconciling reality of Christ, and it invites the world to belong to Christ's community, so that we may be who we are and are becoming in him.

---

84 Torrance, *Resurrection*, 96-8. Although lacking a doctrine of the vicarious humanity of Christ, Heinz W. Cassirer helpfully contrasts Kant and St. Paul. For the former, he argues, moral obligation is self-imposed; for the latter, only committing oneself to Christ frees us from our natural self-centeredness so that we may now love others by the grace of Christ. See his *Grace & Law: St. Paul, Kant, and the Hebrew Prophets* (Grand Rapids: Eerdmans, 1988).

85 Torrance, *Resurrection*, 98f.

Case Issue: Gay Ordination, Marriage, and Rights

One of the emotionally-charged hot buttons of our day is gay rights in the larger culture and gay ordination within the church. As is typical of heated issues, people line up for or against, in opposition or in solidarity, and with polarizing slogans like, "It's natural" or "It's not natural." Unlike this common tendency, Murray Rae and Graham Redding have edited the volume *More Than A Single Issue*, which includes a diversity of Christian scholars who affirm a common faith to overcome such politicized dichotomies. While authors draw various conclusions, this important book represents an attempt to think theologically about an issue that faces the church without letting society dictate the terms of discussion and debate. I will focus on the theological assumptions as represented in a few select essays but not on individual conclusions, for the contribution of this volume is to address a complex issue in light of a trinitarian-incarnational faith and with pastoral sensitivity — irrespective of one's stance on gay ordination. This book may be read profitably in its entirety and for its variety of viewpoints, but I will focus on basic and recurrent theological themes that the church should keep in mind as its addresses gay ordination in particular and gay people in general.

Ray Anderson's theological and pastoral essay bases his discussion on the larger issue of human sexuality: "the intrinsic nature of human personhood as created in the image of God," considering human sexuality "both in the original intention of creation as well as in its fallen and often tragic state." Hence, his discussion of gay ordination begins not with homosexuality but with human personhood and sexuality. If matters of human sexuality are considered biologically rather than theologically, analogous to racial and ethnic status, then "the issue of discrimination, equal rights, and justice become the criteria for deciding the issue."[86]

Anderson's pastoral approach appeals to the "the element of the tragic," for a theology of human sexuality "must include an acknowledgement of the brokenness and tragic aspects of the human sexual experience as well as of the divine intention regarding it." He suggests,

> Whatever one's sexual orientation and practice, be it homosexual or heterosexual, the element of the tragic will always be present.

---

86 Ray S. Anderson, "Homosexuality and the Ministry of the Church: Theological and Pastoral Considerations," in *More Than A Single Issue: Theological Considerations Concerning the Ordination of Practising Homosexuals*, ed. Murray A. Rae & Graham Redding (Adelaide, Australia: Openbook, 2000), 56-7, 60.

> The tragic can mean as little as the temporary frustration of sexual desire when there is no partner available or willing to share it. It can also mean the choice to live in a relationship where sexual relations are impossible, whether due to physiological, psychological or moral reasons. Redemption from the tragic does not guarantee perfect fulfillment of every capacity or desire. It does offer grace to bear with what must be borne, and to sublimate self-gratification in one area to self-fulfillment in another. Every human being is a sexual being and will experience some degree of the tragic in this area.[87]

Anderson discusses the theme of "God's preference" in the realm of human relationships and "God's presence" on behalf of people who struggle amidst confusion and are beset by brokenness. He notes several examples of this theological dynamic in Scripture, such as God's preference for monogamous marriage but his "purposeful presence through the sometimes confusing and problematic social strucure of polygamous marriage" practiced in the Old Testament, even though accommodation to a custom did not make it normative. Similarly, God's preference is that marriage is for life, and he "hates divorce." Yet God's gracious presence upholds those who experience the tragedy of a failed marriage.

"All members of the body of Christ," he observes,

> fall short of God's preference, including homosexual Christians. The Church must be as inclusive as Christ's outreach into human society and as clear headed as Christ's vision of the created purpose for humans as bearing the image of God. Persons with homosexual orientation can receive the Spirit of Christ and become part of Christ's body through forgiveness and mercy the same as those with heterosexual orientation . . . Both preference and presence are grounded in the grace of God, and both alike must be upheld in the teaching and practice of the Church's ministry . . . The Church as the body of Jesus Christ ought to be the place where such struggles and tensions can be experience with the healing power of hope and love.[88]

"When homosexuality becomes a divisive issue within the Church," he concludes, "it has the danger of shifting human sexuality from a possibility to a necessity under the banner of human rights. This attempt to escape

---

87 Ibid., 70-1.
88 Ibid., 72-3.

the tragic by trading what is partial for the whole, will, in the end, prove to be a greater tragedy for us all."[89]

Doug Campbell situates his commentary within the context of Pauline theology and ethics. His "apocalyptic" approach emphasizes "the stark opposition between the two ages or realities": the dichotomies and binary opposition of the old age, such as Jew or Greek, slave or free, male or female, are relative to the new reality in Christ. All the cultural conditions of our humanity, whether race or ethnicity or class or geography and so on — "*all of these are no longer of central relevance to what we are. What matters is the new reality, found in Christ.*"[90]

"Since Christ is at the heart of creation," he notes, "hence redemption will always come first conceptually," which is the biblical and evangelical approach that the church of the triune God should observe in all of its life of Christian community. Hence, gender issues of sexual orientation and preference "*are not defining characteristics of the person or of the Christian*" and do not constitute personhood because being "in Christ" and "in the Spirit" is primary and normative for all people. Over and against "the rhetoric of 'liberation,' which can lead to extraordinary anger, division, coercion and violence" is "a Christian rhetoric" which is "grounded in Christ and the Trinity." "In fact," he concludes, "our salvation in Christ will tell us definitively what we are oppressed by, and to what, and how, we are liberated."[91]

Sue Patterson, like Anderson and Campell, begins with Jesus Christ, who redeems, renews, and transforms creation, and so he is the criterion of what is good. Ethical arguments based on what is "natural" or "unnatural" betray a lack of a Christ-centered definition of what is good and also relies on limited, faulty, and self-interested perceptions. She asserts,

> Unnaturalness, then, is no criterion for rejecting homosexuality on Christian terms. Nor, by the same token, is naturalness a criterion for accepting it. We must step outside of the criterion of naturalness if we are not to attempt to include everything within it. For to take naturalness as primary and then either to grant naturalness to one privileged category of sexual relations,

---

89 Ibid., 76.

90 Douglas A. Campbell, "Some Thoughts on the Apostle Paul and Ethics," ibid., 77-9.

91 Ibid., 89-93.

or instead, conversely, to consider all sexual relations as a level playing field in terms of naturalness is to take a non- or sub-Christian criterion as primary.[92]

She observes the either-or choice of gay Christians. Gay subculture prioritizes "being true to oneself as gay and expressing oneself sexually as such," therefore gay self-identity and pride "take priority over being for God and being true to oneself as called by God to follow Christ." "Given this clash of priorities," she concludes,

> a homosexual Christian will have to choose one or the other, the difference being that homosexual orientation as a biological disposition with relationship consequences will exist whether or not a person identifies as a member of the gay community — one does not have to adopt the condition as a vocation — whereas Christianity is inseparable from membership of the Christian community and cannot by its very nature be compromised by being placed second to another allegiance or perspective. In sum, given the world-embracing nature of both Christianity and the gay subculture, plus the total commitment Christianity claims of its disciples, it may be possible to be both homosexual and Christian if one sits loose to the gay subculture, but not the reverse. As with all areas of human need and appetite, nothing, however compelling and 'natural,' must matter so much as to get in the way of what we are called to be and do as disciples of Christ.[93]

Alan Torrance also lays out a theological perspective to challenge what he considers a static view of human nature, which is to say that our natures "are **fixed** and **unchanging**." "On this view, therefore," he continues,

> the Spirit and participation within the New Humanity of the Body of Christ have and can have no bearing or influence whatsoever on our 'orientations.' Moreover, to suggest that the Spirit might or, indeed, should do so, is interpreted as constituting a destructive anthropological approach by implying that our 'natures' might not be as God intends them to be and that our 'given' self-understandings or self-interpretations may be less than inerrant.

---

92 Sue Patterson, "Nature, Sex and the Cross: Homosexuality and Christian Discipleship," ibid., 129.

93 Ibid., 135-6.

He avers, however:

> The whole thrust of the *imago Dei* metaphor, as it occurs in the Old and New Testaments, serves to stress the fact that the pressure of interpretation in determining the nature of humanity must be *from* God *to* humanity, and emphatically not the other way around. We only know who we are when we *first* know who God is toward us.[94]

He criticizes the "amorphous ideology of the 'natural'" as a common assumption held by proponents and opponents alike who are content to contest whether homosexual orientation or activity is "natural" or "unnatural." "If the *telos* of the created order," however,

> is interpreted in terms of the One who is both creation's author and priest, then it requires to be defined and redefined out of its integrative, ecclesial centre in the One in whom the created order is reordered and fulfilled as the New Creation, the steward of which is not the individual, introspective self but the New Humanity as participants in the Second Adam. This suggests that this *telos* requires to be conceived dynamically in terms of the category of communion — our being created to participate, as creatures, within the communion of the Body of Christ. If this is the case, then a theological definition of 'nature' cannot but make recourse to the triune dynamic which grounds, and determines, and moulds the existence of the contingent order, the 'being' of 'beings.'[95]

Torrance places the burden of proof on those who wish to move beyond the New Testament standard of heterosexual marriage, especially to justify the expansion of such boundaries and the retention of other boundaries. He emphasizes that heterosexual marriage is not invariably "an unambiguous witness and proclamation of God's creative purposes for the New Humanity" since it too exists and functions "*by grace alone, that is, in and through liberated and transformed, creaturely participation in the Body of Christ.*" It is the church's embrace, he concludes, of "a confused, alienated and dysfunctional humanity that must characterise the thinking and all the deliberations of the Body of Christ as it seeks to

---

94 Alan J. Torrance, "Is Homosexuality to be Endorsed Theologically?," ibid., 167-9.

95 Ibid., 174-5.

determine how best it might serve, witness to and live that life offered to the world in the second Adam."[96]

Graham Redding, lastly, acknowledges that people in Christ do not become "a shapeless uniformity and conformity," given that being in Christ does not abolish the particularities of human life. Such diversity of life is a good thing and should not be a basis for division and oppression. And yet, Christ challenges and abolishes these human grounds to perpetuate inequalities and tensions, for in Christ the relativities of life "no longer have an absolute claim" — including the divisive distinctions between homosexuals and heterosexuals that are subordinated and superceded by "the greater unity that is shared by virtue of being in Christ."[97]

Redding concludes by underscoring that human freedom "at its deepest level is derived from the reality of being in communion with God through Christ," which means that the church should challenge "all attempts to define freedom too narrowly in terms of individual rights and personal autonomy." Also, since "freedom is a relational concept, so too are the concepts of sin and righteousness," which compels us to rethink our reliance on moral law and rely on Christ, rather than on "mere compliance with rules and regulations." Therefore, the church should say No both "to those who seek to exalt gay identity in itself and view ordination as a 'right'" and "to those who seek to exalt moral law above the fruits of the Spirit in the task of assessing worthiness for ministry."[98]

In short, the church should be who it is and is becoming in Christ, which means not buying into polarized politics on any single issue. By God's grace, it proclaims and embodies the gospel of Christ's reconciling work in the world, and it witnesses to the Christ who serves his Father in the Spirit on behalf of the alienated, troubled, isolated, distressed, and estranged. Our primary identity is in Christ, which is the church's starting-point for a ministry of grace on behalf of homosexual and heterosexual alike. There is no better place to start than by kneeling together to receive the host and the cup at the altar.

---

96 Ibid., 180-3.

97 Graham Redding, "Being in Christ and Living by the Spirit: A Basis for Understanding Human Identity and Freedom," ibid., 217-20.

98 Ibid., 228-30.

Conclusion

To quote from Markus Barth again, by way of conclusion:

> *There is no wall between the Church and the world!*
> That there *was* a wall between the elect people and the nations is clear, and its removal must not be forgotten. But this wall is gone; it is no more. Christians who would still believe in its existence, or who would rebuild it or protect themselves by something like it, would only be proving themselves hopelessly antiquated, outmoded, outruled, and ridiculous. How could they admire, erect, or use for a shelter that which is 'abolished' and 'abrogated' (2:24f.)?[99]

The Church of Christ, Barth believes, authentically lives in solidarity with the world without pretension or presumption, condescension or tolerance. The body of Christ:

1. serves God in his own work of evangelism and service;

2. "has no other destination and purpose than to live publicly to God's praise";

3. "cannot give anything to the world, unless they receive it, together with the world, always and only from God";

4. witnesses to God in lowliness in the totality of life; and

5. serves nothing less than "the true, full Gospel" of God's grace, truth, and peace.[100]

The Gospel of God's grace is best received as we rediscover the Lord's Supper as an event of Christ's reconciling work of humanity to God and neighbor.[101]

---

99 *The Broken Wall*, 154.

100 Ibid., 165ff.; 171ff.

101 See Markus Barth, *Rediscovering the Lord's Supper: Communion with Israel, with Christ, and Among the Guests* (Atlanta: John Knox, 1988), 59-62.

Chapter 3

A Christological Critique Of Adjectival Theologies

Liberation theology poses social and hermeneutical issues when it asks, "Who is Jesus Christ for us today?" The social question of human and political liberation is a matter to which an incarnational theology cannot remain indifferent, though theology *qua* theology should not be reduced to socioeconomic analysis. The hermeneutical question of the influence of social context and ideology on theology casts suspicion on methodological naivety, though theology *qua* theology is not simply epistemology. While confronting the social and hermeneutical aspects of theologizing, the various theologies of liberation unavoidably raise christological questions and thus require christological critique.

The christological focus within liberation theology is not a uniform or mature development. Gustavo Gutierrez, in his seminal *A Theology of Liberation*, wrote:

> To approach the man Jesus of Nazareth, in whom God was made flesh, to penetrate not only in his teaching, but also in his life, what it is that gives his word an immediate, concrete context, is a task which more and more needs to be undertaken.[1]

The christological task, admitted Gutierrez, had not yet been adequately addressed by liberation theology.

Leonardo Boff undertook the task when he wrote the first liberation christology, *Jesus Christ Liberator*,[2] and Jon Sobrino followed with the more comprehensive work, *Christology at the Crossroads*.[3] The liberation

---

1 Gustavo Gutierrez, *A Theology of Liberation: History, Politics and Salvation*, trans. and ed. Sister Cariad Inda and John Eagleson (Maryknoll: Orbis, 1973), 226.

2 Leonardo Boff, *Jesus Christ Liberator: A Critical Christology for Our Time*, trans. Patrick Hughes (Maryknoll: Orbis, 1978).

3 Jon Sorino, *Christology at the Crossroads: A Latin American Approach*, trans. John Drury (Maryknoll: Orbis, 1978).

christology of Boff and Sobrino needs critical assessment regarding its views on incarnation and reconciliation, as well as its chief concern for liberation. Before considering representative contemporary theologies, however, ancient voices warrant a hearing, especially to guard against modern tendencies to construct theologies based on current concerns and political agendas. An incarnational theology of liberation and reconciliation, based on the vicarious humanity of Christ, shall provide a christological basis for evaluation and critique.

Christological Prolegomena for Liberation and Reconciliation

The double movement of revelation and reconciliation in Jesus Christ, where Christ gives us both true knowledge of God and true life with God, has social implications for liberation and reconciliation. As the Greek and Cappadocian fathers perceived, Christ's assuming of humanity implies the healing of humanity. Jesus "sojourns here as man," writes Athanasius, and "not simply to sojourn here," but also to heal as "the physician" who cures our humanity with his incarnate humanity.[4] Christ bore, as well as cured, our sinful humanity (Matt. 8.17; Is. 53.4; I Pet. 2.24). Christ healed our whole existence, asserts Athanasius, creating reconciliation in a world of war and hate.[5] Christ abolished division and created unity in social relationships (Gal. 3:28; Eph. 2:14ff.; Col. 3:11). The incarnate Christ embraces the whole of human existence, declares Gregory of Nazianzus, in order to sanctify its broken existence, for what God assumes God heals.[6] The Son as the God-Man assumed our fallen flesh to remodel our nature and create us anew. "For that which He has not assumed He has not healed; but that which is united to His Godhead is also saved."[7] God took upon himself human life from birth to death, writes Gregory of Nyssa, healing "all that lies between."[8]

---

  4 Athanasius, "On the Incarnation of the Word," trans. Archibald Robertson, in *Christology of the Later Fathers*, ed. Edward R. Hardy (Phila: Westminster, 1954), 69, 97f.

  5 Ibid., 103, 106.

  6 Gregory of Nazianzus, "Letters on the Apollinarian Controversy," trans. Charles G. Browne and James E. Swallow, ibid., 218ff.

  7 Gregory of Nazianzus, "Letters on the Apollinarian Controversy" in *Nicene and Post-Nicene Fathers* (Second Series Vol. 7): *Cyril of Jerusalem, Gregory of Nazianzen*, ed. P. Schaff and H. Wace (Peabody, MA: Hendrickson, 1999), 438-40.

  8 Gregory of Nyssa, *An Address on Religious Instruction*, ed. and trans. Cyril C.

Gregory of Nyssa lays out the divine logic for the mystery of the Incarnation:

> Our diseased nature needed a healer. Man in his fall needed one to set him upright. He who had lost the gift of life stood in need of a life-giver, and he who had dropped away from his fellowship with good wanted one who would lead him back to good. He who was shut up in darkness longed for the presence of light. The captive sought for a ransomer, the fettered prisoner for some one to take his part, and for a deliverer he who was held in the bondage of slavery ... He submits Himself to the condition of a human body, He enters upon the stage of life by being born, and after passing through each age of life in succession, and then tasting death, at last, only by the rising again of His own body, accomplishes his object...[9]

Almighty God, proclaims Gregory of Nyssa, scandalized humanity through his own plan and project of laying hold of our human nature through his servant life, death, and resurrection in Christ, acting in our place and on our behalf. God saves, heals, and liberates "the whole of humanity" and "the whole human race" in "that concrete humanity which He had taken to Himself," of the "one person" Jesus who assumed, healed, and re-established "the meeting-ground both of life and death." "Now to this, with all candid persons, it were sufficient to reply," Gregory continues,

> that the sick do not dictate to their physicians the measures for the recovery, nor cavil with those who do them good as to the method of their healing; why, for instance, the medical man felt the diseased part and devised this or that particular remedy for the removal of the complaint, when they expected another; but the patient looks to the end and aim of the good work, and receives the benefit with gratitude.[10]

Of course, we may be "angry with the doctors, and wince the pain of incision; but if recovery of health be the result of this treatment, and the pain of the cautery passes away they will feel grateful to those who have wrought this cure upon them ... and the like benefits the great mystery of the Divine incarnation bestows." Gregory continues and concludes:

Richardson, ibid., 304; also 291ff., 304ff.

9 Gregory of Nyssa, "The Great Catechism," *Nicene and Post-Nicene Fathers* (Second Series Vol. 5): *Gregory of Nyssa: Dogmatic Treatises*, ed. P. Schaff & H. Wallace (NY: Cosimo, 2007), 487.

10 Ibid., 489.

> For as they who wash clothes do not pass over some of the dirt and cleanse the rest, but clear the whole cloth from all its stains, from one end to the other, that the cloak by being uniformly brightened from washing may be throughout equal to its own standard of cleanness, in like manner, since the life of man was defiled by sin, in its beginning, end, and all its intermediate states, there needed an abstergent force to penetrate the whole, and not to mend some one part by cleaning, while it left another unattended to. For this reason it is that, seeing that our life has been included between boundaries on either side, one, I mean, at its beginning, and the other at its ending, at each boundary the force that is capable of correcting our nature is to be found, attaching itself to the beginning, and extending to the end, and touching all between those two points.[11]

God's having assumed and sanctified humanity in the humanity of Christ is the reality of liberation and reconciliation. For "the universal Healer," Gregory insists, is the one who unmasks our disease in a more radical way than "the application of the remedial process"[12] — and perhaps more so than putative options and alternatives that claim to be radical, not remedial, in light of the many social injustices that contemporary theologies wish to bring to the forefront of our attention and action.[13]

The incarnation presupposes God's liberating and reconciling presence in and through the vicarious humanity of Christ, in which we must — and *may* by God's grace — participate. Christ "comes from God to be the True Priest," proclaims James Torrance, "bone of our bone, flesh of our flesh"; he stands in solidarity with all humans, bearing our names and injustices on his divine heart, and offering true worship and obedience to God in our place.[14] "Christ does not heal us by standing over against us," continues

---

11 Ibid., 496.

12 Ibid., 498.

13 For a critique of liberation theology from the traditional perspective of "radical orthodoxy," see John Milbank, *Theology and Social Theory: Beyond Secular Reason* (Oxford: Basil Blackwell, 1990); John Milbank et al., *Radical Orthodoxy* (London: Routledge, 1999); and John Milbank and Simon Oliver, *The Radical Orthodoxy Reader* (London: Routledge, 2009). For a critical reply from various liberationist perspectives and theologians, see Lisa Isherwood and Marko Zlomislic, eds., *The Poverty of Radical Orthodoxy* (Eugene, OR: Pickwick, 2012).

14 James B. Torrance, "The Vicarious Humanity of Christ," in *The Incarnation: Ecumenical Studies in the Nicene-Constantinopalitan Creed AD. 381*, ed. Thomas F. Torrance (Edinburgh: Handsel, 1981), 138. For essays that build upon the theology of J. B. Torrance, see *Trinity and Transformation: J. B. Torrances Vision of Worship, Mission,*

Torrance, for he assumes and heals our humanity in his vicarious humanity. Grace not only means that God gives himself to us in Christ, but also that Christ's work in our place and on our behalf provides the perfect response to God. Our participation in him and his work by the Spirit is itself a gift of grace.[15] A theology of grace, based on the incarnation and including the full liberation and reconciliation of humanity, demands development to account for the concerns, without succumbing to the weaknesses, of liberation theology.

The Incarnation as the Hermeneutic of Liberation

The liberation christology of Sobrino and Boff places Jesus on a pathway to liberation. Jesus, writes Sobrino, is "the paradigm of liberation" and "the pathway to liberation"; he is the one who "becomes the Son of God" to show us "the way of the Son, the way one becomes Son of God."[16] The fundamental challenge of Jesus, Sobrino concludes, is "to reproduce his own way of life in oneself and one's life."[17] Boff too views Christ as "the first to arrive at the goal; we will follow him."[18] The imitation of Christ, asserts Boff, does not reduce Christ to a moral category, but connects us to Christ "and allows him to act in us."[19]

Sobrino criticizes the classical theology of descent in favor of a theology of ascent. Ontologically he affirms that the Son became human, but epistemologically he suggests that the "human being, Jesus of Nazareth, becomes the Son of God in and through his concrete history."[20] Jesus opens up concrete paths for other humans, he believes, "to approach and

---

and Society, ed. Todd Speidell (Eugene, OR: Wipf & Stock, 2015). Also see Alexandra Radcliff's *The Claim of Humanity in Christ: Salvation and Sanctification in the Theology of T. F. and J. B. Torrance* (Eugene, OR: Pickwick, 2016) and Myk Habets' "The Fallen Humanity of Christ: A Pneumatological Clarification of the Theology of Thomas F. Torrance" in *Participatio: The Journal of the Thomas F. Torrance Theological Fellowship* Vol. 5 (2015): 18-44.

15 Torrance, "Vicarious Humanity," 141.
16 Sobrino, *Christology*, 37, 105.
17 Ibid., 115.
18 Boff, *Jesus*, 20.
19 Ibid., 221.
20 Sobrino, *Christology*, 338f.

correspond to the Father."²¹ Although he agrees with the orthodox statement that the Son assumed human nature to reveal the Father and to reconcile humanity, he asserts that the primacy of revelation is its being a way to the Father. Sobrino abstracts epistemology from ontology, however, and thus detaches Christ's liberating work from the ontic character of Jesus' relation to the Father. Hence, our imitation of Christ, which he bases on an epistemology of Jesus' ascent to the Father, will ultimately fail, for it throws us back upon our own humanity, rather than Christ's person and work for us.

While Boff and Sobrino view the incarnation as a pathway toward the possibility of liberation, which we must imitate, Ignacio Ellacuría, a liberationist with a genuine incarnational theology, suggests that Jesus realizes his liberating praxis "by revealing the Father in history."²² Ellacuría agrees that the humanity of Christ is our access to the Father, but he also believes that Jesus is the specific "name of God for us, his being-with-us and his being-for us . . ."²³ God thus forms the Church as Christ's body "to be the locale of his presence and the mediating locus of his activity."²⁴

In this way, Ellacuría provides a self-corrective within liberation theology against the notion that Christ is a pathway, principle, or function of liberation which we should emulate by our liberating praxis. He reminds us that Christ is the very being of God with us and for us. The movement of the Father in the Son and by the Spirit is the liberating reality of the incarnate Word for the world, rather than a Christ who has for us merely the *value* of liberation (as a contemporary version of the theology of Albrecht Ritschl). The movement of the Son in the Spirit and to the Father suggests the continued presence of Christ through the body of Christ. The risen Christ implies the ongoing reality of liberation in which we participate, instead of relying upon our own resources to imitate Jesus and "allow" Christ to act through us. In short, the incarnation assumes the being of the Father in the Son through the presence and power of the Spirit for human liberation.

Boff's statement that the liberating praxis of Christ was born "of a profound experience of God"²⁵ should be altered to read: the liberating

---

21 Ibid., 340, 342.

22 Ignacio Ellacuría, *Freedom Made Flesh: The Mission of Christ and His Church*, trans. John Drury (Maryknoll: Orbis, 1976), 58.

23 Ibid., 132, 140.

24 Ibid., 82.

25 Leonardo Boff, "Salvation in Jesus Christ and the Process of Liberation," in *The*

praxis of Christ was based on the reality of Christ's Sonship to God. This is no academic criticism that is indifferent to the presence of sin and oppression in the world. On the contrary, the reality of liberation is assured by the ontological oneness of Jesus with God in Christ's assuming and sanctifying of our humanity. Furthermore, the continued presence of Christ's liberating praxis is guaranteed by the oneness of the Spirit with God and Jesus, for the Spirit is the re-*present*-ation of Christ the Liberator. Hence, my theological criticisms are not based on a commitment to the priority of doctrine over praxis, but arise from a concern for the interrelation of theology and praxis, both grounded in an incarnational theology of grace.

Catholic theologian Roberto Goizueta rightly roots human praxis in the very life and love of God revealing himself and acting through Christ in history:

> The love that God is, and which is expressed in the person of Christ, is the source of and the touchstone for authentic love. Not only does Christ reveal the Trinitarian God in whose image we are created, but through him God invites us to participate in that Trinitarian life.... Far from submerging individuality within a totalitarian unity, the Trinitarian love of God is the source of personhood, which is inherently relational. Inasmuch as human love participates in this Trinitarian love, so too does love give birth to an authentic autonomy and individual freedom, one rooted not in an illusory ego but in the inherent relationality of the person. Much more than an ethical injunction, the development of a just human community is a participation in the Trinitarian community. Social justice, therefore, is not simply the consequence of respect for human dignity, rights, and the common good (though it includes all these); social justice is the consequence of new relationships, beginning with our new relationship with the God who is 'pure relationality'.[26]

"If Christ fully reveals the God-who-is-love as the truth that grounds all human love," Goizueta continues, "and if social justice is a dimension intrinsic to love, then work for justice is itself grounded in the radically gratuitous character of God's love in Christ." Nonetheless, Jesus Christ as

---

Mystical and Political Dimensions of the Cross, ed. Claude Geffré and Gustavo Gutierrez (NY: Herder & Herder, 1974), 84.

26 Roberto Goizueta, "'I Am with You Always': *Caritas in Veritate* and the Christological Foundations of Catholic Social Teaching," in *Jesus Christ: The New Face of Social Progress*, ed. Peter J. Casarella (Grand Rapids: Eerdmans, 2015), 57.

the triune God's self-gift does not suggest a quietist ethic, he insists, but "the most liberating and most demanding form of action" that goes beyond a "self-generated praxis" grounded in a "self-enclosed, autonomous ego" which expressed the "ego's own needs." Instead and by definition, "social justice represents a response to the needs of the other, needs that can only be addressed if they are first received from the other," especially as we listen to victims themselves speaking before we dare join "with the victims in their struggles for justice." For the crucified Christ himself "hears their cries, and joins his cry to theirs."[27]

Goizueta concludes:

> As the outgrowth of God's won love, work for justice thus involves much more than the balancing of abstract rights and duties (though it includes this); justice ultimately involves the reconstitution of relationships. In other words, social justice is less a 'what' than a 'who,' less a set of principles than a network of reconstituted relationships.

Fellow Catholic theologian David Schindler, contributing to the same volume, similarly suggests that the unique role of the church is not to attempt technical and expert opinions to economic problems, whether from the left or the right. Rather, its role is to challenge "the fragmentary vision" of humanity as "*homo economicus*, a vision that wrongly abstracts the economic meaning" of humanity from "the ontological and theological roots" of humanity in Jesus Christ as the personal and self-giving revelation of the triune God.[28]

The incarnation, to recapitulate, as the concrete reality of God's liberating presence from above to below provides a hermeneutical correction to liberation christology.[29] The hermeneutical criterion is Christ as the Son of God, who in the presence and power of the Spirit assumes and

---

27 Ibid., 60-61.

28 David L. Schindler, "The Anthropological Vision of *Caritas in Veritate* and Its Implications for Economic and Cultural Life Today," ibid., 72-76.

29 For a sympathetic overview and well-balanced critique of liberation christology, see Colin J. D. Greene, *Christology in Cultural Perspective: Marking out the Horizons* (Eugene, OR: Wipf & Stock, 2003), ch. 7. Greene charges liberation theology with relying on a "secular notion of emancipation," so that "liberation remains a catchword for socio-political analysis." He sees a recent development, however, in liberation theology "beyond the false utopianism of the early rhetoric of liberation" and toward a more indigenous Latin American christology, which "can radically break with the Enlightenment myth of human emancipation" (211-17).

heals human existence. This christological criterion provides a corrective to liberation christology, which places Jesus on a continuum with us as a common pathway to the Father. A christological critique, however, points the way forward to a liberating praxis based on Christ's praxis, which is not a function of liberation that we must imitate, but a reality in which God summons and permits us to participate. George Hunsinger, a sympathetic critic of liberation theology, suggests that "the precedence given to God's praxis serves to mobilize rather than detract from human praxis" and "may stand as an indication and suggestion of how a theology of liberation might be anchored more securely in a theology of grace."[30]

---

30 George Hunsinger, *Disruptive Grace: Studies in the Theology of Karl Barth* (Grand Rapids: Eerdmans, 2000), 57. I differ with Hunsinger's asserted alliance of "the political solidarity between Barth and the liberationists," especially in opposition to "the neoconservatives on the crucial matter of capitalism" (46, 48). Karl Barth wrote in his *Letters* that his support of "the unjust situation of the workers" in Safenwil led him to become, "In specific cases!" and "in practice a Social Democrat." Christians make political decisions and should form political alliances. Barth adds a significant caveat: "This means in specific cases, in relation to specific points and tasks, they can and should join up with a party which stands for the right thing." See his *Letters 1961 - 1968*, ed. J. Fangmeier & H. Stoevesandt, trans. & ed. G. W. Bromiley (Grand Rapids: Eerdmans, 1981), 303. Also see Barth's discussion of capitalism and socialism in III/4, where he decries the utilitarian treatment of humanity "on a foundation of private capital . . . in the West" *and* of a different form of injustice in "a state socialism which is in fact directed by a ruling and benefit-deriving group" — which "not withstanding its pretended abolition of [capitalist] injustice, might finally amount only to a new and perhaps even crasser form of the oppression and exploitation of man by man. This may or may not be so, but Christianity in the West has its main work cut out to comprehend the disorder in the decisive form still current in the West, to remember and to assert the command of God in face of this form, and to keep to the 'left' in opposition to its champions, i.e., to confess that it is fundamentally on the side of the victims of this disorder and to espouse their cause. It need not on this account identify its message with any of the programmes advanced by these counter-movements. It will wisely refrain from doing so." He carefully qualifies his "left"-leaning politics: "Again it has to be said that the command of God, to the extent that it can and will be heard, is self-evidently and in all circumstances a call for counter-movements on behalf of humanity and against its denial in any form, and therefore a call for the championing of the weak against every kind of encroachment on the part of the strong." Barth stood for solidarity with humanity, especially when weak and exploited such as his parishioners in Safenwil, as relative, provisional, and concrete, but not as "the most radical attempt at reform in the guise of 'revolution,' which can only have relative significance and force. It is again made clear that the root of the troubles lies deeper, namely, in a human aberration which necessarily gives rise to the exploitation of man by man in ever-changing forms — so necessarily that even the most well-meaning and rigorous attempts at counter-movement can arrest and modify but not entirely remove it. . . If man does not allow himself to be kept from forgetting the fellow-humanity without which he cannot be

Christ's Liberation as the Basis for Liberation

The incarnation implies God's assuming, sanctifying, and liberating of the fallen human and created order in Jesus Christ. All things are created and reconciled in him (Col. 1:15ff.). The incarnation of Christ *as* a human being in space and time affirms the wholeness of salvation. Salvation without liberation rests on a partial soteriology that limits Christ's saving work to a religious side of life, and a defective anthropology which divides soul and body. Sin affects humanity, nature, and society; salvation embraces all human, natural, and social life.

A one-dimensional view of salvation, asserts Jan Lochman, whether pietistic escapism or political activism, wrenches apart the two inseparable yet inconfusable beams of the one cross.[31] "Christ's liberation" is thus a basis for reconciliation in two senses: first, Christ liberates us as an aspect of his comprehensive soteriological work, and second, Christ liberates himself beyond the historical particularities of the incarnation to be the Liberator and Reconciler of all peoples through the Spirit of Pentecost.

Two contemporary depictions of Christ as Liberator understand Christ as the "black Messiah" and the "feminist Messiah." The question, "Who is Jesus Christ for us today?" has concrete relevance to black and feminist theologies. More particularly, black theology asks, "Can a white savior save blacks?" and feminist theology asks, "Can a male savior save women?"[32] Several representatives respond to the dual question, Can a white or male savior save blacks or women?

The response is "no" when Jesus is presented as the black Messiah, whether literally (as by Albert Cleage[33]) or symbolically (as by James

---

man, or from pursuing his empty and inordinate desires instead of his genuine and vital claims, his work will necessarily stand under the sign not merely of competition but of exploitation, of open class war, whether in its capitalistic or its socialistic guise." See his *Church Dogmatics*, III/4, ed. G. W. Bromiley & T. F. Torrance, trans. A. T. Mackay et al. (Edinburgh: T & T Clark, 1961), 544f. Finally, see George Hunsinger's *The Beatitudes* (NY: Paulist, 2015) for what could serve as a Christ-centered model for a liberation theology that acknowledges Christ as the center, calls for all people to participate in Christ, and addresses practical contemporary concerns of poverty and injustice.

31 Jan M. Lochman, *Reconciliation and Liberation: Challenging a One-Dimensional View of Salvation*, trans. David Lewis (Phila.: Fortress, 1980), 5ff.

32 For a sympathetic survey and balanced assessment of feminist christology, see Greene, *Christology*, ch. 8.

33 Albert B. Cleage, *The Black Messiah* (NY: Sheed & Ward, 1968), 3f.

Cone[34]), or where the "incarnation" is identified with the contemporary women's movement (as by Mary Daly[35]). "Incarnation," in this negative response, becomes Christ's contemporary solidarity with a particular liberation cause. Although this negative response provides a legitimate critique of lily-white and patriarchal portrayals of Christ, this is its main value: It says "no" based on and bound to a particular cause or social context. This first response thus deploys Jesus as an ideological Christ for the cause of solidarity with the oppressed.

The response of "yes" may present Jesus as the new human, whether as a paradigm of servanthood (as for Rosemary Ruether[36]) or as the representative of true humanity (as for Letty Russell[37]), or as the universal Liberator of black and white (as for Allan Boesak and Deotis Roberts[38]). These theologians understand the incarnate Christ as the liberator of humanity, which implies a more constructive and less exclusive christology than the politicized Christ of those who say "no" to the white and male savior; but they tend to deny or diminish the significance of Jesus' concrete and particular humanity as a male Jew. This second response thus understands Christ as a universal Christ.

A final and preferable response is both "yes" and "no." No, for a christology made in our own image cannot save us, whether black or white, traditional or feminist, liberating or dominating, for the incarnate Christ is not captive to our ideologies of oppression and liberation. Yes, however, for the particular Jewish, male flesh of Christ saves us. The incarnate Christ assumes the sinful flesh of a male Jew, the crucified Christ confronts our fallen nature and nailed it to his cross, and the risen Christ transforms our humanity by his exalted humanity. The particular Christ is the universal Christ. For in his crucified humanity, argues Ray Anderson, he brought the natural (fallen) criteria of race and sex to the cross, and in his resurrected humanity, he has created a new criterion and imperative for human

---

34 James H. Cone, *A Black Theology of Liberation* (Phila.: Lippincott, 1970), 218f.

35 Mary Daly, *Beyond God the Father: Toward a Philosophy of Women's Liberation* (Boston: Beacon, 1973), 96f.

36 Rosemary Radford Ruether, *To Change the World: Christology and Cultural Criticism* (NY: Crossroad, 1981), 35, 43, 54ff.

37 Letty M. Russell, *Human Liberation in a Feminist Perspective — a Theology* (Phila.: Westminster, 1974), 135ff.

38 Allan Aubrey Boesak, *Farewell to Innocence* (Maryknoll: Orbis, 1977), 143f.; J. Deotis Roberts, *Liberation and Reconciliation: A Black Theology* (Phila.: Westminster, 1971), 24f., 138ff.

relationships.[39] Hence, the new humanity of Christ is a critical criterion of judgment and grace, confronting both hierarchical patterns of domination and ideological demands for liberation, and yet presenting itself as the already-present anticipation of the reconciled reality of black and white, male and female, rich and poor.

Theology should not simply be a reflection of our social situation, which is a negative tendency of liberation theology that only repeats the error of the white male theology it rebukes. Although we cannot deny our contextual particularity, neither should we deny the concrete particularity of Jesus, the male, Jewish savior of all humans. The incarnate Christ through the Spirit of Pentecost creates unity and reconciliation among all peoples, nations, and races (Acts 2). Jesus Christ liberates us to be truly human in all our relationships. The risen and ascended humanity of Christ thus radically qualifies our human existence in the world. Christ, therefore, liberates himself from *all* self-imaged portrayals of him. Christ's liberation, over against both a false, spiritualized other-worldliness and a false, secularized this-worldliness, transforms all humans in their concrete contexts by his humanity.

Lesslie Newbigin, a pastor, ecumenist, theologian, and missionary in India, comments on the word "contextualization" as an acknowledgement "that every communication of the gospel is already culturally conditioned." There is no "pure gospel . . . not embodied in a culture." The Bible itself had "a specific cultural setting."[40] We all do theology "from below," not "from above," which "is the illusion of traditional theology." Nonetheless: "The practitioners of the hermeneutics of suspicion are not exempt from its procedures." "Before the cross of Jesus," Newbigin continues, "there are no innocent parties. His cross is not *for* some and *against* others." "The content of the gospel," he proclaims, "is Jesus Christ in the fulness of his ministry, death, and resurrection. The gospel is this and nothing else. Jesus is who he is, and though our perceptions of him will be shaped by our own situation and the mental formation we have received from our culture, our need is to see him as he truly is." "True contextualization," he concludes, "happens when there is a community which lives faithfully by the gospel and in that

---

39 Ray S. Anderson, "The Resurrection of Jesus as Hermeneutical Criterion: A Case for Sexual Parity in Pastoral Ministry" (Parts I and II), *TSF Bulletin*, Jan./Feb., Mar./Apr. 1986; later published in *The Shape of Practical Theology: Empowering Ministry with Theological Praxis* (Downers Grove: IVP, 2001), 77-101.

40 Lesslie Newbigin, *The Gospel in a Pluralist Society* (Grand Rapids: Eerdmans, 1989), 142-4.

same costly identification with people in their real situations as we see in the early ministry of Jesus."[41]

Alan Torrance uses the phrase "cultural foundationalism" to describe the view "that culture defines the necessary form of theological questioning, even though those who advocate this may wish to deny (problematically) that they are conditioning in advance the actual content of their conclusions."[42] While it is true descriptively that "our interpretations of Christ *are and have been conditioned*, as a matter of fact, by our various and diverse contexts," it is an altogether different matter to insist prescriptively that

> christological interpretations *ought to be conditioned* by our context. If it is suggested that they should, the question immediately arises: In what way should this take place and what kind of critical controls operate here? Does our context provide prior conditions which we define in advance and then apply in our interpretations of God's Word to humanity? If so, how do we take due cognisance of the freedom of God whereby God is acknowledged as the one who may re-define and re-order not only the content of our questions but their very form?[43]

Torrance cites Dietrich Bonhoeffer's preference to describe "God's Word to humanity in Christ" as "Counterlogos" rather than "Logos" since the latter title too easily opens the door for us to subsume, categorise, and interpret the Logos under prior categories of thought and with a predetermined agenda. When this occurs, the Logos becomes the ratification, the divine stamp on our world-view — the Logos becomes our own human logos given a capital "L." However, if the Logos is to be taken seriously as the Word of God to humankind, then this Word stands over and against our systems of thought and prior (often subliminally self-oriented and self-interested) cultural agendas and context-conditioned directions of thought. The Word serves, rather, to liberate and to reorientate our world-view, to bring us to new, more inclusive and often more radical ways of interpreting and reinterpreting the world around us. To the extent that this Word stands to transform our agendas and to re-define our questions and interests, this Logos is more accurately described from our perspective as the Counter-Logos.[44]

---

41 Ibid., 149-54.

42 *Christ and Context: The Confrontation between Gospel and Culture*, ed. H. Regan and A. Torrance (Edinburgh: T & T Clark, 1993), 2.

43 Ibid. 4.

44 Ibid. 5-6.

Bonhoeffer believes the question, "Who is Jesus Christ for us today?," is the most basic theological and christological question. "The question, 'Who?,' is the question about transcendence. The question, 'How?,' is the question about immanence." The transcendent God, Bonhoeffer continues, questions us, so that we face the boundary of our own existence. "So the question of transcendence is the question of existence, and the question of existence is the question of transcendence. In theological terms: it is only from God that man knows who he is." Bonhoeffer insists, "Existence cannot emerge out of itself, it remains related to itself and only mirrors itself in itself. Fettered in its own authority it still goes on asking the question, 'How?' The human heart is *cor curvum in se* (the heart turned in upon itself), as Luther says. When we ask, 'Who are you?,' then we speak the language of the obedient Adam, but we think the language of the fallen Adam, which is, '*How* are you?'"[45]

Jürgen Moltmann praises Bonhoeffer's question, "*Who really is Christ for us today?*," in a way that betrays Bonhoeffer's concern to focus on Christ. While rightly criticizing a privatized religion of Christianity — "The crucified Christ has become a stranger to the civil religion of the First World and to that world's Christianity" — his "*social* christology" focuses on an analysis and critique of "scientific and technological civilization." His soteriologically-oriented christology picks as his first target capitalist self-interest, reducing Bonhoeffer's christological focus to a static and simplistic social analysis of an unchanging society and its poor people:

> Technological progress evidently benefits capital, not labour. The productivity of the economy is growing — and unemployment is not diminishing but increasing. A population is growing up which is living below the poverty line, people who are condemned to life-long unemployment, surplus people, who have no part in the wealth of the present, and have no future — people who are not needed. This contradiction too seems more than a passing crisis. It is inherent in the structure of technoloigcal development and in the market structure. "*Who is Christ for these 'surplus' masses of people today?*"[46]

---

45 Bonhoeffer, *Christ the Center* (NY: Harper & Row, 1966), 30-31.

46 J. Moltmann, *The Way of Jesus Christ: Christology in Messianic Dimensions* (San Fran.: Harper, 1990), 63-66, 71. One could also question the appropriation of Bonhoeffer by Reggie L. Williams, who deploys Bonhoeffer on behalf of "the black Christ" in a world characterized by racism, militarism, and white surpemacy. Williams argues that Jesus as *Stellvertretung* (or "empathic, vicarious representative") provides a moral mandate

A Christlogical Critique of Adjectival Theologies

Moltmann wishes to uphold "the unity of christology and christopraxis," but both christology and christopraxis suffer in his socialist critique and eventually are conflated, in his own words: "christology and christopraxis become one." He reduces christology to soteriology and soteriology to social criticism, even while reiterating the refrain: "Who is Jesus Christ for us today?"

Salvation includes Christ's liberating and reconciling work, for Christ liberates us from all forms of bondage and oppression and frees us for transformed social relationships. Christ the Servant, however, remains the Lord of his salvific work, providing a christological critique of adjectival theologies and all forms of anthropocentric and politicized theologies. He takes his own way into human history, the incognito and suffering Jewish man of Nazareth, to heal our humanity, transform society and the cosmos, and reconcile us to one another as Jew and Gentile, male and female, rich and poor and all inbetween, black, white, and all races. Hence, I add another criticism to my christological critique of liberation theology: liberation is authentically Christian when it leads to reconciliation.

Human Reconciliation as the Goal of Liberation

Reconciliation, to agree with liberation theology, should not imply the cheap grace of conciliation. Reconciliation is through the cross and thus includes conflict. There is no shortcut to reconciliation. Reconciliation is not ignoring oppression or placating one's enemies. Reconciliation is not mere integration. Reconciliation is not a question put by the powerful to the powerless, by whites to blacks, or by males to females. Instead, reconciliation implies living in the reconciled reality of the Christ who struggled and sacrificed to remove conflict between us. Reconciliation

---

and model for Christian social action. Bonhoeffer did in fact hear the gospel in black churches of Harlem, which he did not hear at nearby Union Theological Seminary or in mainline white churches (which he described as "Protestantism without Reformation"!). Whether or not the Harlem Renaissaince was the basis for Bonhoeffer's view of Jesus as *Stellvertretung* warrants discussion. See Williams' *Bonhoeffer's Black Jesus: Harlem Renaissance Theology and an Ethic of Resistance* (Waco, TX: Baylor, 2014). Eric Metaxas provides a different viewpoint than the mainline, liberal Bonhoeffer scholars' view of him as a champion of social justice. He interprets Bonhoeffer's experience in Harlem as formative for him as an evangelical theologian. See Metaxas' *Bonhoeffer: Pastor, Martyr, Prophet, Spy* (Nashville, TN: Thomas Nelson, 2010). As we read various appropriations and misappropriations of Bonhoeffer, we should keep in mind the self-critical query, "*Who really is Bonhoeffer for us today?*"

affirms *response*-ability, that is, responding to one another within the reality of Christ's reconciling work by the presence and power of the Spirit.

Reconciliation, on the other hand, does not equate political liberation with the Kingdom of God, conflate reconciliation and revolution, or reduce reconciliation to the fulfillment of a demand made by the powerless to the powerful, by blacks to whites, or by females to males. Separatism is not an adequate alternative to integration, for it too can forsake the social reality and implications of Christ's reconciling work. God's Kingdom does not rest on political activism, no more than on political quietism. Human causes do not effect or contribute to the realization of God's Kingdom. Instead, reconciliation implies participating in God's action in Christ, who freely sets up his Kingdom. Reconciliation affirms transformation, that is, human change, both individual and social, based on the re-creative work of God between his first and final coming.

The Christian church which proclaims the message of reconciliation must practice the reality of reconciliation in all of life, such as multi-ethnic churches which encourage neither the guarding nor the grabbing of power but a parity of participation in Christ's work to liberate and reconcile the world. Humanity *is* concretely limited by our relative but dangerously divisive historical differences of race, sex, class, culture, and caste. This historical reality, notes Karl Barth, creates "very different assumptions, questions, anxieties, needs and tasks," but God sanctifies historical existence and summons us to historical responsibility.[47] The establishment of Christian fellowship, declares Barth, must neither remove nor sanction differences, but it should transcend, relativize, enclose, and challenge divisions by being the new people of God which unites the different peoples of the world. Barth comments, for example, on the acute racial question:

> That Churches which are not prepared to settle this question within themselves in the only possible way should have the audacity to engage in missionary work with hope of success is something which can only cause us astonishment.[48]

Christians, both black and white, must work *for* all as brothers and sisters and never in a "friend-foe relationship."[49]

---

47 Karl Barth, *Church Dogmatics*, III/4, ed. G. W. Bromiley and T. F. Torrance, trans. A. T. Mackay et al. (Edinburgh: T & T Clark, 1961), 294f.

48 Karl Barth, *Church Dogmatics*, IV/3, ed. G. W. Bromiley and T. F. Torrance, trans. G. W. Bromiley (Edinburgh: T & T Clark, 1962), 899f.

49 Karl Barth, *The Christian Life: Church Dogmatics*, IV/4 Lecture Fragments, trans.

A Christlogical Critique of Adjectival Theologies

Willie Jennings' *The Christian Imagination* begins with a welcome call to theologians in the academy "to think *theologically* about their identities," especially based on "the central trajectory of the incarnate life of the Son of God, who took on the life of the creature, a life of joining, belonging, connection, and intimacy." Such "a Christian intellectual posture," he suggests, should lead to "transformations not only of ways of thinking but of ways of life that require the presence of the risks and vulnerabilities associated with being in the social, cultural, economic, and political position to be transformed." He charges, however, that "the Christian theological imagination was woven into processes of colonial dominance" and became encased "in racial logics and agency . . ." "Western Christian intellectuals," he continues, "still imagine the world from the commanding heights . . . imagined by Western, white, male identities . . . ," which resist "the realities of submission, desire, and transformation." He tells "the story of modern Christianity's diseased social imagination" as "a theological problem in order to suggest a way forward."[50]

Although Jennings does not view "the theological language of reconciliation" as "irretrievable," he does warn "of its terrible misuse in Western Christianity and its tormented deployment in so many theological systems and projects." Hence, talk of "reconciliation" tends toward "(a) ideological tools for facilitating the negotiations of power; or (b) socially exhausted idealist claims masquerading as serious theological accounts." He does not think "most Christians are ready to imagine reconciliation." So he engages in "theological analysis of theology's social performances — in hopes of articulating a vision more faithful to the God whose incarnate life established and establishes the contours, character, and content of Christian theology." He supports and promotes "cosmopolitan citizenship," which "imagines cultural transformations that signal the emergence of people whose sense of agency and belonging breaks open not only geopolitical and nationalist confines but also the strictures of ethnic and racial identities."[51]

While Jennings does provide a distinctive theological account of race and a transformative social imagination,[52] a reliance on the

---

G. W. Bromiley (Grand Rapids: Eerdmans, 1981), 210f.

50 Willie James Jennings, *The Christian Imagination: Theology and the Origins of Race* (New Haven: Yale, 2010), 7-9.

51 Ibid., 9-11.

52 Ibid., especially in much of ch. 6, where he discusses Israel as the prehistory of the incarnation, of Jesus the Jew.

ideological rhetoric and adjectival theology of our day mars his otherwise impressive book. He directs his critique, for example, against "white space and literacy,"[53] "whiteness,"[54] "nationalism" and "capitalism,"[55] and "the fragmenting of place as private property and the slicing of human existence in racial vision" — that is, the imagination of "race" and "space."[56] "If whiteness became the facilitating reality," he summarizes, "as that form of identity inside of which all other identities could be imagined, then walking away from or renouncing or questioning existence with white identity is no simple matter."[57] His theological analysis which begins with the incarnation finally degenerates into matters of geography and economics: "discipleship" as "global real estate" and "new possibilities of living arrangements" or a "spatial reconfiguration" that announce a move beyond "market desire" and "private property."[58] Such utopian collectivist arrangements unfortunately define his understanding of Christian community, whose proper basis and end is the union and communion of God and not the demolition of capitalism.

Daniel Hardy helpfully notes the etymology of the word "context" (Latin: *contexere*) is *not* to divide and confront but to "'braid,' 'weave' or 'connect.'" Similarly, "culture" is not "fixed and self-enclosed" but "dynamic and intertwined with others," which is where "God in Christ is present" and where "we may further effect the consequences of this presence."[59] "We can embrace others, and be embraced," Hardy continues, "in ways quite beyond our imagining — and there continue to be enlarged by the nearness of God's love. That is the fundamental pattern by which, in the interweaving of human beings and cultures, the presence of God is found. It is the way in which the love of God is continued amongst us who are so sharply separated."[60]

Given contextuality as the interweaving of humans with their cultures, Hardy rightly asserts that

---

53 Ibid., 207-09.
54 Ibid., 228.
55 Ibid., 233.
56 Ibid., 250.
57 Ibid., 275.
58 Ibid., 287, 289, 294.
59 *Christ and Context*, 22-3.
60 Ibid., 41-2.

> the Trinitarian activity of God sustains a complexity of particularities, establishing 'relativities' with their own integrity in fully contextual interweaving. This is to be sharply distinguished from the post-modernists' notion of particularisim, which opposes a false universalism with a false particularism. Their notion of particulars rests on privileging, and the supposition of the inaccessibility of others with whom we are interwoven/contextually related. The active sustenance of the Trinitarian God of a complexity of particularities is also to be distinguished, if I may say so, from those who suppose that becoming indigenous requires severance from others, especially those considered outsiders. These are over-statements, understandable for those who need to recover their particularity from submersion in a monolithic world, but fundamentally a denial of the wider interweaving with contextuality involves.[61]

An incarnational theology of liberation and reconciliation, to agree with Hardy, suggests a connecting and interweaving of peoples and cultures that conform to the new humanity of Christ and confront the sinful racial relations of the world, especially beginning with ourselves, our families and friends, and our churches. The crucified Christ breaks down barriers and dividing walls of hostility (Eph. 2:14), liberating Jew and Gentile, slave and free, male and female, to be one in Christ (Gal. 3:28), to become the reconciled people we are by the Spirit of Christ. The liberationist theologies of our day, whether or not one agrees with their premises and conclusions, do call us to consider our response to the Gospel in concrete faith, repentance, and obedience.

The concrete implications of an incarnational theology of liberation and reconciliation must be worked out in theory and practice in the full dimensions of human existence: suprapersonal (historical and sociopolitical), interpersonal (social and relational), intrapersonal (individual and psychological), and infrapersonal (natural and environmental), which I will address in the next chapter. Liberation theologies confront us with the suprapersonal dimensions of sin and salvation, and rightly so, for sociopolitical structures are bound up with human existence. A theology of liberation and reconciliation, however, should address the multifarious dimensions of human existence, including individuals and their relationships, as well as society and the environment. The "ecopersonal" reality of human existence, rather than unidimensional

---

61 Ibid., 252-3.

analyses, implies responsibility to and transformation of the structural, social, personal, and natural spheres of human existence.

The failure to participate in the reconciled reality of human existence in Christ indicts us with a summons to social repentance. Social repentance does not suggest a legalistic or guilt-ridden response to politicized demands for liberation. It signifies instead a response to the Gospel of Christ, who graciously confronts us with *his new humanity*. Social repentance, which is evangelical rather than legal, presupposes the Gospel of Christ, who is the reality of true humanity and the true basis for our lives as fully human.

Chapter 4

A Trinitarian Ontology Of Persons In Society

Otherwise orthodox Christians, Rahner declares, are "almost mere monotheists," isolating the dogma of the Trinity from any personal relevance to their lives.[1] The doctrine of the Trinity appears in the Church's creeds, prayers, rites, and hymns, but the faithful must often wait until Trinity Sunday to hear the significance of the Trinity for their identity as Christians. Likely, they will hear imperatives without indicatives, moral mandates devoid of ontological grounding in God's grace. No wonder the the laity often ignore the triune God amid their life and work in society, given his perceived lack of relevance in many churches.

This neglect of the Trinity, Moltmann warns, can lead to the merely moral activism and pragmatic thinking of what he terms "moral monotheism."[2] Instead, a trinitarian ontology — God's being as a union and communion of persons — provides a firmer footing for personal relations in society and holds together the unity and diversity of humanity. "[T]he Triune God," suggests Alan Torrance, "is both active within the whole sphere of human contextuality and, furthermore, has being in and through this dynamic engagement."[3] "For God's identity does not rest on 'being out-side,'" notes Daniel Hardy, "but on who he is in what he does, on his being in his acts."[4] A trinitarian ontology of personhood derives "ought" from "is": Because God is a preeminently tripersonal being, humans created in God's image must, and may, live as persons in relation to God, other persons, and the world.

---

1 Karl Rahner, *The Trinity* (New York: Seabury, 1974), 10, 14.

2 Jürgen Moltmann, *The Trinity and the Kingdom* (NY: Harper & Row, 1981), 8f.

3 *Christ and Context: The Confrontation between Gospel and Culture*, ed. H. Regan & A. J. Torrance (Edinburgh: T & T Clark, 1993), 6.

4 Ibid., 23.

A Perichoretic Paradigm of Persons in Relation

There is no greater need today than to treat persons as persons. The Church's distinctive task in society includes upholding persons as bearers of God's image. The Church may be a model for society when it reflects what John of Damascus called the perichoresis of God's being: the reciprocal giving and receiving of free communion between Father, Son, and Spirit. Jesus prays for all believers to indwell the mutual love and knowledge and fellowship of Father and Son as the ground for their unity and as a witness to the world (Jn. 17:20ff.).

A "paradigm" (Gk. paradeigma = "pointer") of the personal points to an analogical[5] relationship between God and humanity: that humans find their true being in relation to others mysteriously reflects the very being of God. God's triune life of communion, God's being-as-communion, is the basis and reality of human life. A perichoretic paradigm, an important theme in recent trinitarian theology, emphasizes: God in us, we in God, and we in one another.[6] The tripersonal God shares his divine life of communion with humans so that humans may live as a union of persons in communion with God and one another.

The concept of "person" denotes to some "the modern notion of subjectivity" — psychological individuality that leads to a tritheistic understanding of God.[7] Rahner suggests instead the phrase "distinct

---

5 The tendency of feminist theology, by contrast, rejects the univocity of a logical model and accepts the equivocation that often reacts to it. Even Sallie McFague's "metaphorical" theology — "true but not literal," over and against the "idolatry" and "irrelevance" of "hierarchical, authoritarian, patriarchal models of Western theology" (univocity) — equivocates. "God the father," she believes, "is a profound metaphor and as true as any religious model available," but the "hegemony of paternal models must be supplemented with maternal, as well as nonfamilial and non-gender-related ones" (such as "God as friend"), because of the "discontinuity, skepticism, and relativity between our language and its reference to God and the world" (*Metaphorical Theology: Models of God in Religious Language* [Phila.: Fortress, 1982], 28f., 145, 178, 194). For a theologically illuminating treatment of God-language that both reaffirms and complements the tradition by suggesting the phrase "Motherly Father," see the Church of Scotland's report, *The Motherhood of God*, ed. A. E. Lewis (Edinburgh: St. Andrew, 1984).

6 See especially Catherine Mowry LaCugna, *God For Us: The Trinity & Christian Life* (San Fran.: HarperCollins, 1991); Colin E. Gunton, *The Promise of Trinitarian Theology* (Edinburgh: T & T Clark, 1991); *The Forgotten Trinity*, 3 Vols (London: British Council of Churches, 1989-91); Leonardo Boff, *Trinity and Society* (Maryknoll, NY: Orbis, 1988); John Zizioulas, *Being as Communion: Studies in Personhood and the Church* (NY: St. Vladimir's Seminary, 1985); Moltmann, *The Trinity*.

7 Rahner, *The Trinity*, 112f.

manner of subsisting," even though he considers it "a quite formalistic concept" that "says very little about Father, Son, and Spirit . . ."[8] (Kasper criticizes his concept as not kerygmatically or doxologically meaningful, which he says is "Rahner's primary concern." Aside from its increased likelihood of unintelligibility, he charges, "no one can invoke, adore and glorify a distinct manner of subsisting."[9])

"Person in relation" more adequately conceives of the mutual loving relations of the triune God and humanity created in the image of God. God is not, asserts Kasper, a "static substance" or a self-contained being but "being-from-another and being-for-another." Because humans analogically reflect the imago Dei, he continues, important anthropological implications follow: they are not self-sufficient or autonomous individuals but those who live "humanly only in I-Thou-We relations."[10]

A "person," Gunton agrees, differs from an "individual": the latter is separate from other individuals; the former is in relation with other persons. Persons are free for a "mutually constitutive relationship with other persons" — genuine others who must not violate one another's particularity. They are not individual substances that enter into personal relations but are "made what they are" by personal relations.[11] No mere logical difficulty, the triune God is a communion of persons. The Trinity signifies, LaCugna rightly asserts, not a "self-contained relationality," but she wrongly reduces the triune God to "God's life with us and our life with each other."[12] [T]he God of the Gospel, Barth better notes, "is no lonely

---

8 Rahner, *The Trinity*, 109, 112f. Also cf. Karl Barth's phrase "mode of being" in his *Church Dogmatics*, I/1 , 2nd ed., ed. G. W. Bromiley & T. F. Torrance & trans. G. W. Bromiley (Edinburgh: T & T Clark, 1975), 363.

9 Walter Kasper, *The God of Jesus Christ*, trans. Matthew J. O'Connell (NY: Crossroad, 1986), 288.

10 Ibid., 280, 290.

11 Gunton, *Trinitarian Theology*, 10f., 156.

12 LaCugna, *God For Us*, 103, 228. Paul Molnar strongly and rightly criticizes how LaCugna has "collapsed the immanent into the economic Trinity," erased "a clear distinction between Christ and us," and has paralleled Feuerbach's conception that "universal love" makes someone a Christian and even "Christ himself." See his incisive critique in *Faith, Freedom and the Spirit: The Economic Trinity in Barth, Torrance and Contemporary Theology* (Downers Grove: 2015), 24 (including n. 4), 45, 393f. (including n. 19). Also see his earlier work, *Divine Freedom and the Doctrine of the Immanent Trinity: In Dialogue with Karl Barth and Contemporary Theology* (NY: T & T Clark, 2005), for a full-scale critique of the modern tendency to reduce the immanent to the economic Trinity based on human experiences projected onto God in lieu of God's self-revelation to

God, self-sufficient and self-contained," for he is free to be "more than the personal (or impersonal) 'wholly other.'"[13]

God is not the impersonal, mechanistic one of Enlightenment Deism but persons in relation who freely indwell one another and graciously grant a contingent (i.e., relative but real) human freedom for community. God's being as communion — triune and yet one, truly other and yet related — is the ontological ground for human unity and community.[14] The triune God, T. F. Torrance suggests, gives humans a contingent personal existence out of the fullness of his personal being — creating "personalised persons" who are healed and restored in relation to God and others.[15]

God's being as personal communion raises the question whether the world is a suitable place for persons qua persons. Because personhood constitutes being itself, humans created in God's image must challenge societal arrangements that depersonalize humans. Individualism and collectivism — "mirror images of one another" — both signal the loss of the person.[16] Individualism or pathological freedom, Gunton avers, denies "humanity to those unable to 'stand on their own feet.'" Collectivism or abstract equality denies the differentiation necessary for genuine community. Otherness and relation, he summarizes, are "correlatives rather than rivals."[17]

John Macmurray's *Persons in Relation* criticizes both individualism and collectivism by developing the thesis: "the Self is constituted by its relation to the Other" — i.e., it has its being in personal relationship. The "Self and Other are correlatives," he contends; they only exist as persons in mutual relation to others.[18] Personal communion and action are his central emphases: "Our human Being is our relations to other human beings . . . Our relation to God is itself real only as it shows itself in our

---

us, which is the only true basis for human freedom and liberation.

13   Karl Barth, *Evangelical Theology* (Grand Rapids: Eerdmans. 1963), 10.

14   Gunton, *Trinitarian Theology*, 39, 99, 132f.

15   Thomas F. Torrance, *The Trinitarian Faith* (Edinburgh: T & T Clark, 1988), 230f. For a discussion of Torrance's trinitarian soteriology, see Dick Eugenio, *Communion with the Triune God: The Trinitarian Soteriology of T. F. Torrance* (Eugene, OR: Pickwick, 2014).

16   Gunton, *Trinitarian Theology*, 88ff., 92, 99.

17   Ibid., 117, 133, 171.

18   John Macmurray, *Persons in Relation* (NY: Harper & Row, 1961), 17, 86, 211.

relation to our neighbours."[19] The theological question, he asserts, is not, "Does God exist?" but "Is what exists personal?"[20]

LaCugna likewise criticizes both individualism and collectivism in favor of a personal-social-relational understanding of humanity based on the Trinity. She approvingly (and astoundingly) affirms, however, what she calls a feminist slogan: "the personal is the political."[21] (This problem, as we will see below, is especially evident in Boff's thought, who also criticizes the twin evils of individualism and collectivism but clearly perceives individualism as the greater evil.)

Discussions of community as personalizing agents in impersonal societies risk the danger of idealizing such communities. Macmurray defines a community as "the unity of persons" that retains both individuality — the other is genuinely other — and mutuality of relation (including equality of intention, rather than de facto equality). A community, he continues, accepts "the inherent ideal of the personal . . . a universal community in which each cares for all and no one for himself.[22] The Church, Zizioulas similarly believes, as a eucharistic and an eschatological community has the proleptic capacity "to love without exclusivism" and to transcend the exclusiveness of natural and social ties and "all divisions."[23]

A trinitarian-incarnational realism — rather than the idealism that Macmurray normally rejects — grounds the hope of human unity and community in the reality of Christ. He is the one sent by his Father in the Spirit to offer his life and death on behalf of the many. Macmurray's Harnackian God offers no ontological basis for the personal-communal relations for which he pleaded throughout his life.[24] Even Zizioulas'

---

19 John Macmurray, *Search for Reality in Religion* (London: Friends Home Service Committee, 1969), 72.

20 Macmurray, *Persons in Relation*, 215. We must "conceive a personal universe in which God is the ultimate reality," he amplifies, a world created by God and created agents endowed "with a limited and dependent freedom" (222, 224; also see his *The Self as Agent* [NY: Harper & Row, 1957]).

21 LaCugna, *God For Us*, 288; emphasis mine.

22 Macmurray, *Persons in Relation*, 158f. Macmurray also believes that the Church must cooperate with God to establish his kingdom on earth, and even writes of its role "to save the world" by transforming human motives through love (*Search for Reality*, 76f).

23 *Being as Communion*, 57f., 254f.

24 See his *Search for Reality* as a summary and culmination of his mature religious thought. His early traditional Scottish Calvinist beginning and his temporary alliance with Baptist and Brethren associations led to a disillusionment with traditional religion.

emphasis on the Church's eucharistic communion makes too direct a link between God and the Church, bypassing the vicarious humanity of Christ as the one who graciously permits humans to participate in his life of unbroken communion with his Father in the Spirit and for the many whose broken relations he heals.[25]

Humans find their true being as a communion of persons whose mutual, personal relations mirror, however imperfectly, the triune life of God. While affirming a perichoretic paradigm of persons in relation, I will develop an "ecopersonal" critique of the many gospels of liberation that separate or confuse the personal, social, and natural matrices of being human that reflect the unity and plurality of God. I intend to balance individuality and community, or diversity in unity, so that the Church's life in society indirectly mirrors the being of the triune God.

An Ecopersonal Paradigm of Persons in Society

A paradigm of the personal, ontologically grounded in the tripersonal God, provides a critique of the many social programs that often, even if unintentionally, depersonalize people. (Consider the American welfare state's enslavement of some people in a cycle of dependence, helplessness, and hopelessness that destroys personal values and [disproportionately black] families, despite the best of intentions to "help" the poor. The many "liberation" theologies of our day should expose the paternalistic pretensions of such statist solutions). My ecopersonal paradigm suggests an ecological model of the personal as dynamically related to the social and natural context of human life, which I will discuss within the context of personal life.[26] I have called the four interrelated (unitary yet differentiated) dimensions of life "suprapersonal," "interpersonal," "intrapersonal," and "infrapersonal." Many contemporary liberationist gospels separate or confuse these realms that exist "above," "between," "within," and "below" persons.

Despite his central emphasis on personal communion, he lived his religious life as an isolated individual. Despite his critique of theoretical idealism, he only found a spiritual home among the Society of Friends after his retirement from teaching philosophy.

25 See James B. Torrance, "The Vicarious Humanity of Christ," in Thomas F. Torrance, ed. *The Incarnation: Ecumenical Studies in the Nicene-Constantinopolitan Creed* (Edinburgh: Handsel, 1981), 127-47.

26 Cf. the traditional but unfortunate academic distinction between "personal" and "social" ethics.

A Trinitarian Ontology of Persons in Society

First, the suprapersonal dimension consists of the structures and institutions of human life, the sphere of life that Macmurray describes as "persons in indirect relation." The political goal is to maintain justice: "the minimum of reciprocity and interest" in personal relations. This bond of society, rather than a community of persons in direct relation, relies on the state as a useful and necessary device to deal with exceptional breaches of trust and cooperation. For the indirect, functional relations of society (united for a "common purpose") cannot produce the personal relations of community (united for a "common life"). He warns, however, against personifying or absolutizing the limited and impersonal state, not insisting that it "hand us the millennium on a platter."[27]

Liberation theologians, for example, advocate utopian projects to free the oppressed from "unjust" (invariably capitalist) societies. Leonardo Boff attempts to ground his liberationist perspective on the triune God. He believes the traditional trinitarian models emphasize unity at the expense of diversity. The Greek model protects the unity of God by starting with the person or monarchy of the Father; its danger is its subordinationist tendency. The Latin model preserves the unity of God by beginning with the unity of the divine nature; it tends toward modalism. He advocates what he calls a third way: the perichoretic communion of the Trinity — that is, the mutual love and knowledge, life and freedom, and interpenetration of the divine persons in, by, with, through, and for one another. While this model tends toward tritheism,

---

27 Macmurray, *Persons in Relation*, chs, 6, 9; *Conditions of Freedom* (London: Faber & Faber, 1949), 54f. Macmurray's early optimism toward synthesizing Christianity and Marxism still regarded Christianity as the truer belief, but Marxism as the superior alternative to the Fascist menace of the time (see his *The Philosophy of Communism* [London: Faber & Faber, 1933]; *Creative Society: A Study of the Relation of Christianity to Communism* [London: Student Christian Movement Press, 1935]; and "Christianity and Communism: Toward a Synthesis," in John Lewis, Karl Polanyi, & Donald K. Kitchen, eds., *Christianity and the Social Revolution* [London: Gollancz, 1935], 505-26). His ambivalence toward even democratic socialism is evident during this period. Democracy demands socialism, he believed, to ensure economic democracy (equality, as well as freedom); yet socialism erodes (political) democracy, for the government control of the economy expands the role of the presumed "omnicompetent" state (see his *A Challenge to Churches: Religion and Democracy* [London: Regan Paul, 1941], 32f.; *Constructive Democracy* [London: Faber & Faber, 1944], 11ff.). Late in his life, he shifted even greater responsibility to the church, whose "main task is to become a *real* community in the world," practicing love and unity and freedom that "cannot be produced by the compulsion of law and organization, by any form of socialist or communist power" (*Search for Reality*, pp. 78f.; also cf. his critique of communism as deifying the state and depersonalizing its citizens, despite its noble intentions in *Self as Agent*, 30).

he supports its overall balance of unity and diversity, a bond of communion that he claims nonetheless values individuality and accepts differences.[28]

He faults both capitalist and socialist societies as impersonal systems that fail to reflect the trinitarian communion in society. The former system, he generalizes, upholds the rights of isolated individuals "divorced from any consideration of their relation to society." It protects "the dictatorship of the property-owning classes" and excludes majorities from the production process, justifying the triumph of the one over the many. "Such regimes," he alleges, "have produced the greatest divisions in history" between classes, races, and sexes. Most third world poverty, he simplifies, results from capitalist greed."[29]

Socialist societies, he believes, have the "right principle, that of communion between all and the involvement of all in the means of production"; but their collectivist and bureaucratic tendencies swallow up individuals and do not produce equality.[30] He still believes, however, in a perichoresis of economic, political, and symbolic (i.e., values and meaning) structures as "inseparable" — i.e., "always" containing one another, reflecting the mutual interdependence of the three divine persons. This society or community — unlike Macmurray,[31] he makes no distinction — may exist "without conflicts," placing "the common good" above "individual good." It will favor "participation and communion of all in everything"; sharing goods in common; "justice and equality for all."[32] Despite Boff's theological framework, however, he often reverts to liberation slogans that supplant a realistic discussion that evaluates which societies actually liberate (i.e., outcomes vs. intentions; cf. the Greek etymology of Utopia: ou + topos = "no place," not eu + topos = "good place").

Novak alternatively defends pluralistic democratic capitalism — combining a political democracy, market economy, and pluralistic culture — as morally, theologically, and realistically superior to all existing political

---

28 Boff, *Trinity and Society*, 4ff., 44ff., 77ff., 93, 232ff.

29 Ibid., 78, 148f.

30 Ibid., 150f.

31 Even during Macmurray's early enchantment with communism, he was wary of the collectivizing nature of bureaucratic structures: "Now serving society or humanity always means in practice serving institutions . . . And the more you serve institutions the more complicated they become, and the more service they demand . . .' (*Freedom in the Modern World* [London: Faber & Faber, 1932], 200). He also asserted: "But serving people in general usually means serving nobody in particular" (ibid., 215).

32 Ibid., 107f., 116, 130, 134, 151, 236.

economies. Each of its three components, he claims, has a relative autonomy — in contrast with Boff's latent collectivism — and yet an interdependence that provides mutual restraint. Novak converts, however, the perichoretic relations of Father, Son, and Spirit into an abstract principle of "pluralism-in-unity" when he views pluralistic democratic capitalism as mirroring the Trinity in society.[33] Novak does not differ in principle from Boff's de facto method of directly applying trinitarian principles to society; he simply disagrees with his brand of political economy. Nevertheless, his defense of capitalism merits consideration when one reads the anti-capitalist bent of the many politicized theologies of our day.

Democratic capitalism's realistic spirit, Novak argues, acknowledges sin and the unintended consequences of even the noblest aims; hence, it resists the bureaucratic imposition of statist ideals upon other sectors of society and prefers the more effective and dynamic distribution of relative goods — not "the Good" — through the market (i.e., creating wealth to reduce poverty). Yet its moral-cultural base does not permit the rampant individualism of free enterprise alone. It encourages the formation of many communities (for the individual and the state are not the primary entities in society). Pluralistic mediating communities (e.g., families, churches, synagogues, schools, and voluntary associations) instruct individuals in virtue and provide an alternative to rugged individualism and utopian collectivism.

Next, the interpersonal realm comprises social relationships, rather than the dichotomy of private individuals who secure meaning and value for themselves and public megastructures that alienate people from personal existence. Mediating communities are institutions that mediate between the private and public spheres, the "people-sized institutions" of moral authority where people generate and maintain values. Because they have both private and public faces, they can give private life stability and public life meaning.[34]

The concept of mediating communities encourages a dynamic sense of pluralism against both an ideal, inclusive community that somehow transcends exclusiveness (the integration model, analogous to modalism) and the cynical sanctioning of racial division (the separation

---

33 Michael Novak, *The Spirit of Democratic Capitalism* (NY: Touchstone, 1982), 337ff.

34 Peter L. Berger and Richard John Neuhaus, *To Empower People: The Role of Mediating Structures in Public Policy* (Wash., D.C.: American Enterprise Institute for Public Policy Research, 1977), 2ff.

or self-segregation model, analogous to tritheism). Instead of separationist and integrationist models, the nation must sustain a dynamic balance of unity and plurality that respects the racial, regional, religious, and other distinctives that constitute a unified society.

While government rightly proscribes racial discrimination, for example, it oversteps its bounds when it prescribes numerical balancing of the racial composition of schools.[35] The state should permit parents to make basic choices in the key area of their children's education, rather than disenfranchise (especially lower-income) parents by the state's coercive and virtually monopolistic role in education. Whether children attend a neighborhood school or are bussed across town should primarily be a family and not a governmental decision. Enforced "integration" will not create the personal relations necessary for the healing of race relations. Macmurray decries the confusion "to think that the problems of society . . . are problems of political and economic organization," for they are "problems of community — that is to say, not political but religious problems."[36]

The Church as a community of persons that reflect the tension and balance of the tripersonal God must avoid mathematical and impersonal models of community that opt for either unity or diversity.[37] Modalistic ideas of God parallel an overemphasis on unity: "integrated" churches (schools, neighborhoods, etc.) that often fail to appreciate the particularity of one's background (unity as uniformity). "Integration," de-emphasizing diversity, requires the many to conform to the one. At Pentecost, by contrast, the Spirit enabled the community to speak in other languages, not one (heavenly or earthly) language. The many were amazed that they heard God's wondrous acts in their native tongues.

Tritheistic notions of God parallel an overemphasis on diversity: "ethnic" churches that absolutize otherness at the expense of relation

---

35 Ibid., 14f.

36 Macmurray, *Religion, Art, and Science: A Study of the Reflective Activities in Man* (Liverpool: Liverpool Univ., 1961), 68. He also argues that genuine community requires an internationally and interdenominationally inclusive Church (*Search for Reality*), 80; yet mutual "I" and "You" relations respect otherness (*Reason and Emotion* [London: Faber & Faber, 1935], 222). Once again, however, he lacks a trinitarian ontology to ground the plurality-in-unity of social relationships.

37 Gunton warns that "relation without otherness" will result in a "blank homogeneity" or bland unity, but "otherness without relation" tends toward an "irrational pluralism" (*Trinitarian Theology*, 172f.). Also cf. Pascal: "Multiplicity which is not reduced to unity is confusion. Unity which does not depend on multiplicity is tyranny" (quoted in Kasper, *God of Jesus Christ*, 291).

(diversity as divisiveness). Cone, for example, does not even support personal relations between blacks and "white oppressors."[38] He dismisses (his fellow black liberationist) Roberts' criticism of his rejection of reconciliation with whites as "a white criticism," or simply what whites want to hear.[39]

The liberationist work Doing Theology in a Divided World also illustrates an overemphasis on the multiplicity of social contexts as its way of doing theology.[40] Despite the claim that this plurality of perspective is somehow "interdependent," one wonders how theologies of liberation can commonly speak of the one Gospel of Jesus Christ. Christ — who lived, died, and rose as the one on behalf of the many — speaks to and in cultures. He liberates all — whether black or white, Asian or Hispanic, rich or poor, male or female — from speaking of him in their own image; and he reconciles all to be who they are and are becoming in him as multifarious peoples.

Dinesh D'Souza has chronicled the "politics of race and sex on campus" in his Illiberal Education, a narrative of his firsthand interviews with administrators, faculty, and students in American colleges and universities. "Diversity, tolerance, multiculturalism, pluralism — these . . . are the principles and slogans of the victim's revolution."[41] Remedies to alleged structural or institutional racism, sexism, and homophobia include preferential admissions policies based on race, gender, and sexual orientation; curricular changes that oust European and heterosexual "white male" classics of Western civilization (Homer, Aristotle, Shakespeare, and other "DWMs" — "dead white males") and require study of non-Western and minority cultures to "liberate students from ethnocentrism"; and a campus life that fosters diversity and in some instances mandates sensitivity training and consciousness-raising. D'Souza ironically reports a heightened bigotry and self-segregation at such schools. Intending multicultural diversity and ethnic harmony, they have instead achieved separatism, intolerance, and an illiberal education that enslaves rather than frees persons. A genuine pluralism in schools, he counters, would

---

38   James H. Cone, *God of the Oppressed* (San Fran.: Harper & Row, 1975), 241.

39   J. H. Cone, *My Soul Looks Back* (Maryknoll: Orbis, 1986), 61f.

40   Virginia Fabella and Sergio Torres, eds. *Doing Theology in a Divided World* (Maryknoll, NY: Orbis, 1985).

41   Dinesh D'Souza, *Illiberal Education: The Politics of Race and Sex on Campus* (NY: Free Press, 1991), 17.

encourage intellectual diversity and base affirmative action admission policies on socio-economic disadvantage instead of race,[42] which is to say, to appreciate people as individual persons, not merely as group members.

Next, the intrapersonal aspect of humanity suggests psychological individuation or the distinctive otherness of human persons. Individuals are persons in relation but not merely parts of a system.[43] The merger of persons in a marriage indicates a pathological marriage. (Even Adam had a prior relationship with God, creation, and [despite his loneliness] himself, before entering into relationship with Eve.) The merger of persons with an omnicompetent state presumes the state can achieve social and moral ends more fitted to persons.

Individuality, however, can easily lapse into individualism. In distinguishing a person from a mere individual — which could easily be organized in a collective society — as having a right and vocation to be different, Novak writes,

> A democratic capitalist society mirrors the infinity of God through the conflicting, discordant, irreconcilable differences of huge numbers of persons, each of whom is an originating agency of distinctive insight and distinctive choice.[44]

Persons in relation who mirror the triune God do have a capacity for choice and freedom, but Novak's overemphasis on the hypostases of divine and human persons — the "irreconcilable differences" — does not the mirror the triunity of God.

Contemporary Western culture tends toward a narcissistic preoccupation with the self.[45] "Selfism" proclaims the Gospel of self-esteem, self-fulfillment, self-help, or self-worship. These are the superficial slogans

---

42 Ibid., 20f., 229ff., 251ff. He quotes Arthur Schlesinger: "the melting pot has yielded to the Tower of Babel" (quoted on 238).

43 Cf. Woody Allen's movie *Zelig* (Orion, 1983) as a satire on the modern loss of selfhood. Leonard Zelig (Woody Allen), a human chameleon, assumes the personality and appearance of anyone he associates with, whatever their race, size, profession, or creed happens to be (e.g., he blends his fragile self into a mass rally for Adolf Hitler). Zelig recovers a genuine sense of otherness only as he develops a romantic relationship with his psychiatrist, Dr. Eudora Fletcher (Mia Farrow).

44 *Democratic Capitalism*, 64.

45 See the incisive theological analysis and critique of this phenomenon by Alan J. Torrance. "The Self-relation, Narcissism and the Gospel of Grace." *Scottish Journal of Theology*, Vol. 40 (1987), 481-510. Also consider the "New Age" movement as a union of Eastern pantheistic monism and Western deified selfism.

that supplant any substance to discussions of the self. The ethical relativism of much moral education leaves moral persons no firm footing to speak on behalf of moral values and against immorality or injustice. Individualistic forms of psychotherapy put one on a quest to discover "what's right for me,"[46] even if that violates the covenantal commitment to one's marriage. (Contrary to the commonplace pronouncement that "the family is in decline," in fact, high divorce rates indicate idealistic expectations for marriage and a consequent inability to "settle for unsatisfactory approximations" of one's so-called "ideal mate."[47])

An egocentric view of the self, Macmurray correctly criticizes, views the world as a means to the private satisfaction of individual ends, not for its own sake.[48] "Real thought and feelings," he counters, "are about the real

---

46 Walker Percy alternatively subtitles his whimsical *Lost in the Cosmos: The Last Self-Help Book*: "How you can survive in the Cosmos about which you know more and more while knowing less and less about yourself, this despite 10,000 self-help books, 100,000 psychotherapists, and 100 million fundamentalist Christians" (NY: Washington Square, 1983), 7. For an introduction to the British object relations school, which counters individualistic psychology with a social-relational understanding of the self, see Eric Rayner, *The Independent Mind in British Psychoanalysis* (London: Aronson, 1991).

47 Brigitte Berger and Peter L. Berger, *The War over the Family: Capturing the Middle Ground* (Garden City, NY: Anchor, 1984), 166. Cf. Woody Allen's *The Purple Rose of Cairo* (Orion, 1985), in which Tom Baxter (Jeff Daniels) — an "archaeological explorer" — literally steps out of the movie to become a real self who experiences the reality of love and personal relations with Cecilia (Mia Farrow), who also faces the dilemma of choosing between fantasy (movies) and reality (relationships with real people, however unsatisfactory they might be). For theological essays on marriage and family, see Kettler and Speidell, *Incarnational Ministry*, chs. 15-21. For sound advice on cultivating the emotional bonds of marriage that counters the common myth that "communication" (beginning with the formulaic "I feel") is the key to a successful relationship, see Sue Johnson, *Hold Me Tight: Seven Conversations for a Lifetime of Love* (NY: Little, Brown, 2008) and *Love Sense: The Revolutionary New Science of Romantic Relationships* (NY: Little, Brown, 2013); similarly see John Gottman and Nan Silver, *The Seven Principles for Making Marriage Work* (NY: Harmony Books, 1999, 2015) and John Gottman and Julie Schwartz Gottman, *10 Lessons to Transform Your Marriage* (NY: Three Rivers Press, 2006).

48 Macmurray, *Reason and Emotion*, 52. Trevor Dobbs has written on John Macmurray's foundational influence upon Harry Guntrip and the whole school of object relations psychology. He writes, "What Guntrip would later jointly pursue with Fairbairn in the remaking of Freudian metapsychology was the redemption of the emotional "id" experience as *unruly* and portending *disaster* to that of a hungering after attachment to the object that was the experience of meaningful aliveness." He adds, "It is a false dichotomy that thoughts are *rational* and feelings are *irrational*, secondary and subordinate to cognitions." See his "John Macmurray as a Philosophical Basis for Harry Guntrip's Object Relations Theory" in Todd Speidell, ed., *On Being a Person: A Multidisciplinary Approach to Personality Theories* (Eugene, OR: Wipf and Stock,

world and in terms of its realities. If you cut yourself off in any way from the life around you, your own reality is lost, and with it your freedom."[49]

A heterocentric or "objective" view of the self understands the center of human (including emotive) activity as outside oneself, oriented to the other instead of one's "subjective" feelings. Yet Macmurray's immanentist, non-trinitarian, non-incarnational view proclaims "total self-transcendence," "a complete 'personal objectivity' in which 'I am nothing, and you are everything.'"[50] Only in Christ may we say, "I no longer live, but Christ lives in me," and therefore "I live by faith in the Son of God, who loved me and gave himself for me" (Gal. 2:20). While God does give the human subject its "proper place," T. F. Torrance avers, we find our true humanity in union with Christ, not in "our subjective fantasies," "a gross personalism," or "anthropological statements."[51] Christ alone has healed the sinful preoccupation with selfhood to liberate, not negate, the self for God and others.[52]

Even worship can become the discovery of one's own deity, not the praise and proclamation of the triune God known in Jesus Christ.[53] Naomi Goldenberg, for example, advocates what she calls religion as psychology: "feminist witchcraft," conceiving "its deity mainly as an internal set of images

---

2002), 110, 112. Also see Dobbs' "John Macmurray's Influence on Object Relations Psychology" in Speidell, ed., *On Being Christian and Human* (Eugene, OR: Wipf and Stock, 2002), 206-23, and *Faith, Theology, and Psychoanalysis: The Life and Thought of Harry S. Guntrip* (Eugene, OR: Pickwick, 2007). Finally, see Daniel J. Price, "Discovering a Dynamic Concept of the Person in Object Relations Psychology and Karl Barth's Theology" in Speidell, ed., *On Being a Person*, 125-45, and his *Karl Barth's Anthropology in Light of Modern Thought* (Grand Rapids: Eerdmans, 2002).

49 Macmurray, *Freedom*, 206f. Again, persons exist in relation, especially to friends as "the essence of morality" (ibid., 209). Macmurray would eschew any Platonic ideal of friendship, of course, in favor of acting on behalf of real friends.

50 Macmurray, *Religion, Art and Science*, 37, 58.

51 Thomas F. Torrance, "The Distinctive Character of the Reformed Tradition," in C. D. Kettler & T. H. Speidell, eds., *Incarnational Ministry: The Presence of Christ in Church, Society, and Family* (Colorado Springs: Helmers & Howard, 1990), 5ff.

52 Also consider Allan Bloom's critique of American nihilism and his own Platonic idealism as both lacking a trinitarian-incarnational realism as an ontological basis for personhood (see his *The Closing of the American Mind: How Higher Education Has Failed Democracy and Impoverished the Souls of Today's Students* (NY: Simon & Schuster, 1987).

53 For a trinitarian-incarnational view of worship that criticizes anthropocentric views of worship, see two articles by James B. Torrance: "The Vicarious Humanity of Christ," in T. F. Torrance, ed., *The Incarnation*; and "The Place of Jesus Christ in Worship," in Ray S. Anderson, ed., *Theological Foundations for Ministry* (Edinburgh: T & T Clark/Grand Rapids: Eerdmans, 1979), 348-69.

A Trinitarian Ontology of Persons in Society

and attitudes." "The prominence of a female divinity in all forms of witchcraft," she continues, "fosters psychological strength in all female witches." Goddess religion allows "individualism," she unabashedly announces, for "each woman is considered a Goddess," each "the priestess of her own religion."[54]

A trinitarian basis for feminism, LaCugna counters, supports a relational instead of an autonomous view of the self that values mutuality, community, and interdependence. She rejects both individualism and collectivism, though, like Boff, she faults individualism with greater frequency and severity. While she bases her feminism on a perichoretic understanding of personal diversity in communion — "permeation without confusion" — she reverts to a modalistic emphasis on unity by advocating total equality and androgyny (gender as prosopon). Jesus, she asserts, has overcome "the antinomies of maleness and femaleness," for his personhood "embodies the perfections of both male and female." God created persons, she continues, "to be inclusive of . . . everything and everyone else, past, present, and future."[55] For LaCugna, modern egalitarian notions of equality compete with her understanding of unity as a genuine diversity of persons in communion. Are maleness and femaleness simply "antinomies" to be overcome in Christ? Or does gender differentiation analogically reflect the very mystery of the ontological differentiation of the Trinity? While nature does not determine personhood, sexuality does embody our lives as God's covenant creatures. As Elaine Storkey suggests,

> Both our spirituality and our sexuality can therefore be redeemed. We can shake free from the pagan influences of our culture and from the brokenness in our relationships because Christ has died to release us from the bondage to sin. And that bondage is yet more powerful when it is the bondage of a whole society, rather than the struggles of any one individual. We can turn from our worship of the creature rather than the Creator, and deveop a spirituality which centres on God rather than that which centres on ourselves.[56]

---

54 Naomi R. Goldenberg, *The Changing of the Gods: Feminism and the End of Traditional Religions* (Boston: Beacon. 1979), 89ff. She also writes that "male witches are considered Gods," but women have a higher position in the power structure" (103). Evidently, for this radical feminist, matriarchy, not equality, is the antidote to patriarchy. Jesus fares no better, for "psychoanalytic theory suggests that the image of an antiseptic male god cast in the role of savior could very well be a symptom of the direction toward death which human culture seems to have taken" (106).

55 LaCugna. *God For Us*, 267ff., 281f., 290.

56 Elaine Storkey, "Spirituality and Sexuality," in D. W. Torrance, *God, Family and Sexuality* (Eugene, OR: Wipf & Stock, 1997), 155.

Lastly, the infrapersonal side of life encompasses nature or the environment. The early chapters of Genesis clearly place God's covenant with humanity in the context of a creation that he calls "very good" (1:31). In stark contrast with Platonic dualism, "God created the heavens and the earth" (1:1) militates against an other-worldly escape hatch to leave this evil earth. In contradiction to romantic pantheism, however, God created only humans in his image and gave them dominion over the earth (1:26). A dynamic tension exists between otherness and relation, even between humanity and nature.

Moltmann distorts the twin themes of sociality (interpersonal) and stewardship (infrapersonal) that constitute the imago Dei by advocating a monistic utopianism. The Trinity, according to him, unites not only "individuality" and "sociality" but also "Western personalism" and "Eastern socialism": a community of people in relation to one another, not the gods of "power and possession."[57] He believes liberated people would realize "the Good" of an "unequivocal world" — "one with each other, one with nature, and one with God" — against "this ambiguous world of possessive individualism." The "love and solidarity" of such liberation — to "become personal and authentically social" — implies quite literally, he concludes, the "abolition of property."[58] Christian Kettler aptly responds: Moltmann is "beholden to abstract anthropocentric principles" instead of the dynamic, personal relations of the triune God.[59]

God created the earth as an arena for personal creativity, social cooperation, and harnessing the means of human nourishment, enjoyment, and betterment. The dynamic model of creating wealth — in contrast with the static model of redistributing wealth — can inspire persons, families, and cultures to labor as God's stewards. Stewardship of God's creation entails the possession and production of goods for the sake of human community: what parents give to their children (often quite sacrificially rather than "individualistically"); what neighbors give — materially as well as personally — to others in need; what churches and voluntary associations give to their communities. The laity have a special role in teaching the beneficiaries of help how to invest themselves personally, creatively, and productively as stewards of God's creation.

---

57 Moltmann, *The Trinity*, 198ff.

58 Ibid., 214ff.

59 Christian D. Kettler, *The Vicarious Humanity of Christ and the Reality of Salvation* (Lanham, MD: Univ. Press of America, 1991), 90.

Stewardship also implies care for the earth. Ironically, and at the risk of being "politically incorrect," capitalist creativity does not simply contribute to the ecological crisis, but also provides a means and motive to produce environmentally sound technology. While Moltmann may label inventors, manufacturers, and distributors of such technologies as "possessive individualists," they can help avert anti-business policies that may cost workers their jobs. Personal creativity can be one way to serve God and nurture his earth.

My ecopersonal critique has suggested that the many social, political, and liberationist theologies of our day fall short of preserving the personal. Some of these ideologies overemphasize one sphere of life over another — e.g., liberation theology's primary focus on structures (suprapersonal). Others conflate different spheres — e.g., Moltmann's monism of humanity (interpersonal and intrapersonal) and nature (infrapersonal). A more fundamental failure abandons the distinctive theological task of perceiving and witnessing to the triune God in modern life and instead starts anthropocentrically: "doing theology" based on one's social context, individual needs, or ideological demands. "[T]he many reductionistic theological programs" today, Kasper challenges, should once again take up "theological theology"! — returning to theology's proper theme, especially in light of pressing human need.[60]

Contemporary discussions of civil rights and multicultural diversity illustrate the pressing need to preserve the personal. Rather than pit one group against another, a genuinely pluralistic society will encourage persons to be persons in relation to institutions, others, themselves, and nature. Neighborhoods, families, and churches have a special capacity to sustain personal relations in society.

The church, urges J. B. Torrance, should set aside its vested interests for a ministry of reconciliation, in which

> it is the duty of the Christian church on the one hand to listen to the Word of God, the gospel of grace and reconciliation, but on the other to listen to the cry for justice of the poor, the exploited, and the oppressed, to fulfill our prophetic function in the world by seeking to give to all their humanity — in seeking love, justice, and freedom for all.[61]

---

60 Kasper, *God of Jesus Christ*, 15, 316.

61 James B. Torrance, "The Ministry of Reconciliation Today: The Realism of Grace," in Kettler & Speidell, *Incarnational Ministry*, 137.

Christian ministry and service, notes G. W. Bromiley, is not a human prerogative, for "speaking human words or performing Christian acts, whether in worship, a church program, or personal service," is Christ's ministry and service. We can "trivialize" Christian ministry, he warns, or "reduce it to human terms . . . with its own possibilities of service and advancement." "We can take a humanitarian stance . . . to further human betterment, to challenge and correct abuses, to promote progressive insights, to provide relief for human misery." The Spirit of Christ continues Christ's presence and work, so that the church may minister in his name as they speak his Word and do his acts.[62]

A trinitarian ontology of persons in society affirms the public example and witness of the Church as a theological agent of social witness and criticism. The Church as a mediating community should uphold persons qua persons in the full context of human life and existence, not merely in a privatized side of life. The Church's mission, essence, and goal may reflect the triune God in society by questioning depersonalizing models of human relations that simply opt for unity or diversity, individualism or collectivism, integration or separation. In pointing the way toward more personal relations in society, it may reflect the very being of the triune God, not only on Trinity Sunday but also in the nation.

Conclusion

A return to the weekly celebration of Holy Communion as a means toward multiracial and multidenominational reconciliation would begin to earth the Church's faith in the God of Jesus Christ. The Spirit of Christ may use the Church in his "ministry of reconciliation" as "Christ's ambassadors" to the world beyond the Church; therefore, Paul concludes, "Be reconciled to God" (2 Cor. 5:18ff.). The Church that intends to proclaim the message of reconciliation — that God has graciously destroyed the dividing walls of ethnic, religious, and cultural hostility (Eph. 2:8ff.) must itself practice the reality of reconciliation, for in Christ the Church may "become a dwelling in which God lives by the Spirit" (2 Cor. 2:22).

---

62 Geoffrey W. Bromiley, "The Ministry of the Word of God," ibid., 79, 82.

Chapter 5

The Humanity of God and the Healing of Humanity

"Social justice is not an abstract principle, nor is it an ideal to be pursued. Social justice is the core of human experience. It is bread and water; it is blood and bones; it is brothers and sisters who unlearn the knowledge of how to hurt and how to kill and who learn to live in the power, the freedom, and the hope with which God intended that we should live. If there is any theological basis for social justice, it lies between us, within our humanity; it is anthropological. Social justice is a divinely ordained order of human existence . . . Social justice flows not from the justice of God as an abstract principle but from his humanity as an historical and continuing power of reconciliation. It is not God's justice but his humanity that is our hope."

Ray S. Anderson, *The Shape of Practical Theology*

The Church's service often presupposes a theology of mission that is "secular" or "spiritual" but too rarely Christian. Where Christians dualistically divorce the sacred and the secular, the theological and the ethical, the Gospel announces that the Word assumed and healed our humanity. All people receive their human dignity in Christ, who forms communities in society based on the love of the Father for humanity and the presence of the Spirit in the world.

The Church, T. F. Torrance asserts, confronts a twofold temptation when facing the stark reality of human need. On the one hand, the institutionalization of worldly power poses a utilitarian temptation to secure success via political lobbying, which naturally requires that one develop social, political, and economic clout of one's own. On the other hand, the authorization of a spiritual retreat poses an otherworldly temptation to abdicate responsibility for social needs by yielding social concerns to the power structures of the state. In either case, Torrance warns, "Christ clothed with His Gospel has been kept apart from Christ clothed with the need and plight of men."[1]

The Christian Church must heal within itself this division of "Christ clothed with His Gospel" and "Christ clothed" with desperate human need. Being in Christ means following the One sent by the Father in the Spirit by participating in his life of worship, mission, and service. The One whom we follow, James Torrance notes, "is a whole Christ," not "a *nudus Christus*." Jesus comes to us, Torrance proclaims, "as our Brother Man, to be our great High Priest, that He might carry on His loving heart the joys, the sorrows, the prayers, the conflicts of all His creatures, that He might intercede for all nations as our eternal Mediator and Advocate . . ."[2] Jesus comes from God as "the True Priest, bone of our bone, flesh of our flesh" — healing us by assuming "that very humanity which is in need of redemption," so that "our humanity is healed *in him*."[3]

In *On The Incarnation of the Word* St. Athanasius says of Jesus: "He has yet of the loving-kindness and goodness of His own Father been manifested to us in a human body for our salvation."[4] God "gave us freely, by the Grace of the Word, a life in correspondence with God."[5] Jesus alone, "being Word of the Father," could "recreate everything," "suffer on behalf of all," and "be ambassador for all with the Father." As "Artificer of everything," he prepared the womb of "the Virgin as a temple unto Himself," assuming our very nature to stand in our stead and offer his life and death to the Father for us, turning us away from corruption and restoring us to incorruption and life.[6] Like a great king who enters a city and resides in a house there, so too "God the Word of the all-good Father" becomes one with us, clothed with our corruption, and renews us to life in his risen humanity.[7] He who "was the Image of the Father" took upon

---

1 Thomas F. Torrance, "Service in Jesus Christ," in *Theological Foundations for Ministry*, ed. Ray S. Anderson (Grand Rapids: Eerdmans, 1979), 730.

2 James B. Torrance, "The Place of Jesus Christ in Worship," ibid., 348, 367.

3 James B. Torrance, "The Vicarious Humanity of Christ," in *The Incarnation: Ecumenical Studies in the Nicene-Constantinopolitan Creed*, ed. T. F. Torrance (Edinburgh: Handsel, 1981), 138, 141.

4 *The Nicene and Post-Nicene Fathers* (Second Series Vol. IV): *St. Athanasius: Select Works and Letters*, ed. Archibald Robertson (Grand Rapids: Eerdmans, 1978), 36.

5 Ibid. 38.

6 Ibid. 40.

7 Ibid. 41.

The Humanity of God and the Healing of Humanity

himself our dying and corrupted humanity and restored and renewed it in the image of God.[8]

Why the incarnation? St. Athanasius answers:

> Now, if they ask, Why then did He not appear by means of other and nobler parts of creation, and use some nobler instrument, as the sun, or moon, or stars, or fire, or air, instead of man merely? Let them know that the Lord came not to make a display, but to heal and teach those who were suffering. For the way for one aiming at display would be, just to appear, and to dazzle the beholders; but for one seeking to heal and teach the way is, not simply to sojourn here, but to give himself to the aid of those in want . . . the Physician and Saviour . . . to cure the things that were. For this cause, then, He has become man, and used His body as a human instrument.[9]

Ray Anderson illustrates the importance of the incarnation by telling the story of a Roman Catholic woman who went into a Christian bookstore and desperately asked for a cross. As a good Protestant bookstore, it only carried naked, barren crosses. "Yes, I'm looking for a cross," the woman commented, "but do you have one with the little man on it?" Anderson adds, "And a cross without its humanity is a cross without its power of reconciliation." He continues,

> But the truth of the gospel is not that humanity has been put on the cross; it is rather that the cross has been sunk deep into humanity. The incarnation has the cross on it before the incarnate One hangs on the cross. More stupendous than the thought of a crucified God is the self-giving and suffering love of the humanity of God. More powerful and more effective than an instrument of death is the instrumental means of reconciliation through incarnational presence in life. More significant than the cross as a religious symbol is the power released through the bearing of the cross under the already inspired witness of resurrection and healing.[10]

The novelist Walker Percy portrays a hospital chaplain Percival, who took the "religious" name Fr. John when he became a priest but who is unsure of

---

8 Ibid. 43.

9 Ibid. 59-60.

10 Ray S. Anderson, *The Shape of Practical Theology: Empowering Ministry with Theological Praxis* (Downers Grove: InterVarsity, 2001), 315f.

the power and presence of God. He visits his old friend Lancelot, who is in a psychiatric prison for murdering his adulterous wife. It is Lancelot who summons and questions this pastoral counselor:

> Yes, I asked you to come. Are you a psychiatrist or a priest or a priest-psychiatrist? Frankly, you remind me of something in between, one of those failed priests who go into social work or 'counseling,' or one of those doctors who suddenly decides to go to the seminary. Neither fish nor fowl . . . So something went wrong with you too. Or you wouldn't be here serving as assistant chaplain or substitute psychiatrist or whatever it is you're doing. A non-job.[11]

My older brother, David, attempted suicide many years ago before his eventual untimely death. Tormented by paranoid delusions that his loved ones were against him and by schizophrenic withdrawal and hallucinations, he was psychologically debilitated to the point of utter despair. My mother, of non-expressive Scandinavian heritage, trained at Moody Bible Institute, and married to an ordained Baptist minister, confessed after this terrible incident that she could no longer pray. (Consider the two false options in the prologue of Job[12] — to praise God for suffering or to "[c]urse God and die!" [Job 1:21; 2:10 in The New English Bible]). As a seminary student at the time studying with Ray Anderson, and reflecting upon the years of coping with the despair of schizophrenia, I could only think to share with her Dietrich Bonhoeffer's powerful line from prison, "Only a suffering God can help."[13] She said, "That's profound, though I'm not sure I fully understand it."

---

11   Walker Percy, *Lancelot* (NY: Ivy, 1977), 3ff. Fr. John does convert from being a comfortable Catholic and half-baked psychologist by the end of the novel. Lancelot and Fr. John represent a Kierkegaardian "either-or": Lancelot advocates an ethical utopia without faith to combat the malaise that underlies a purely aesthetic existence and Fr. John represents the mystery of faith in a godless world. Lancelot challenges the priest's newly found faith: "So you plan to take a little church in Alabama, Father, preach the gospel, turn bread into flesh, forgive the sins of Buick dealers, administer communion to suburban housewives? . . . Very well. But you know this! One of us is wrong. It will be your way or it will be my way" (23ff.).

12   I have included my essay "God, Woody Allen, and Job" as Appendix B.

13   Dietrich Bonhoeffer, *Letters and Papers from Prison* (NY: Collier, 1971), ed. Eberhard Bethge, 361. Also, Walker Percy's protagonist in *The Thanatos Syndrome*, Dr. Thomas More, who practiced psychiatry before he went to prison, perceptively comments, "Sometimes I think that is the best thing we shrinks do, render the unspeakable speakable" (NY: Ivy, 1987), 17.

The Humanity of God and the Healing of Humanity

The Church must develop theological instincts and not simply good intentions, for its service is to God, not to the world. It is God who sends his Son into the world and who has graciously given to the Church a distinctive service to God: namely, to be human with others before God. Because God has restored to us our true humanity in Christ, the Spirit leads the Church to re-present the One Christ in whose face we may see the loving heart of the Father for the world.

"The incarnation did not 'Christianize' humanity," Anderson observes; "it 'humanized' humanity." By implication, he infers,

> No longer can sexual status, economic status or racial distinctives be used as criteria for relationship with God or for seeking advantage over others; The incarnation was not for the purpose of putting the humanity of God on the cross but for the purpose of sinking the cross deeply into human life. When God 'dies' on the cross, what is put to death is all that is inhuman in humanity.[14]

Humans may now freely respond not only to God as Father but also to others as brothers and sisters. The many social, political, and liberationist theologies of our day would do well to heed Anderson's admonition that what both the Church and world desperately need is nothing less than the humanity of God as the basis and reality of our own created and restored common humanity.[15] As Karl Barth observes, "On the basis of the eternal

---

14 *Shape of Practical Theology*, 139, 157.

15 Cf. the "progressive Marxist" and "revolutionary Christian" posture of Cornel West, who advocates the alliance of "black theological reflection and action . . . rooted in the progressive Marxist tradition . . ." (*Prophesy Deliverance: An Afro-American Revolutionary Christianity* [Phila.: Westminster, 1982], 106) — though any kind of theological reflection recedes into the background of his later *Race Matters* (NY: Vintage, 1933). In his *Prophetic Fragments*, West advocates "interpreting the Christian faith in light of our present circumstances," set against the caricatured alternatives that he perceives and poses: "transcendental reflection on the nature of morality" or "historical mimicking of the liberal tradition." The Christian faith, according to his *a priori* political ideology, "must lead to some form of democratic and libertarian socialism" (Grand Rapids: Eerdmans & Trenton, NJ: Africa World, 1988), 130, 134. Also cf. J. Moltmann, who more theologically upholds a trinitarian theology over and against what he calls a mere "moral monotheism," but he too resorts to socialist abstractions when he advocates, for example, the "unity of everything" and the "abolition of property" (*The Trinity and the Kingdom: The Doctrine of God* [San Fran: Harper & Row], 1981), 216f. For a powerful and penetrating critique of such "anthropocentric theologies," see Christian D. Kettler, *The Vicarious Humanity of Christ and the Reality of Salvation* (Lanham, MD: Univ. Press of America, 1991), especially ch. 5, "The Humanity of God as Critique of Anthropocentric Theologies."

will of God we have to think of *every human being*, even the oddest, most villainous or miserable, as one to whom Jesus Christ is Brother and God is Father; and we have to deal with him on this assumption."[16]

The Church's social mission should not reduce needy people to sociological abstractions, such as "the poor," "the disadvantaged," or other labels that enable us to evade personal relations with our neighbors in need. Anderson perceives in Karl Barth's concept of neighbor a radical solidarity of cohumanity in Christ, in whom both "near and distant neighbors" confront us with "the concrete existence of the other" as the context for ethical reflection.[17] "Christian ethics," then, should not baptize the abstract duties or principles of deontological ethics nor the calculations and consequences of utilitarian ethics nor even the emphasis on character in virtue ethics. Instead, God commands us to live in concrete responsibility to one's neighbors as fellow human beings created, loved, and redeemed by God.[18]

God lives and reveals himself as a union and communion of Father, Son, and Spirit. The Father sends the Son in the Spirit both to reveal God's heart for the world and to reconcile the world unto God. The Spirit of the incarnate, crucified, risen, ascended, and coming Christ leads us into worship, communion, mission, and service. Churches that neglect this trinitarian basis for human life are left bereft of a message, of any hope of witness, mission, or service, and of a reality of human community and reconciliation that is rooted in God himself.

The Scottish philosopher John Macmurray, who began his personal pilgrimage in the Church of Scotland and later supplanted traditional religious practice with a quasi-Marxist faith, always believed that Christianity was superior to Marxism in its understanding of community. The state can at best coerce, and at worst depersonalize, its citizens without producing the personal relations that characterize Christian community. Modern western philosophy, too, lacks a proper commitment to personal communion and agency, focusing instead on isolated individuals contemplating the world.

---

16 Karl Barth, *The Humanity of God* (Atlanta: John Knox, 1960), 53.

17 *Shape of Practical Theology*, 146ff.; also see 161ff. for a discussion of the "Sociocultural Implications of a Christian Perception of Humanity."

18 I have surveyed these four ethical traditions, based on duty (deontological ethics), consequences (utilitarian, egoistic, and altruistic ethics), character (virtue theory), and God's commands (Divine Command Theory), in my *From Conduct to Character: A Primer in Ethical Theory*, 4th ed. (Eugene, OR: Wipf and Stock, 1998). See Appendix A for a radio interview I did related to this book and to selected social issues of the time from an evangelical perspective.

The Cartesian thinking self withdraws from others to contemplate ideas, thus separating reflection from action and persons from communion. Despite Macmurray's central emphasis on personal communion, he ironically lived his religious life as an isolated individual, and only later in life did he find a real sense of Christian community among the Society of Friends that his earlier Marxist faith could never realize.[19]

Macmurray's philosophy of community — namely, that persons are who they are in relationship to others, and that these relationships are necessarily and preeminently personal[20] — sorely needed a real basis and ontological antecedent for personal relations. Abandonment of the Trinity can only lead to moral and political imperatives detached from the indicatives of the triune God's being of love, grace, and freedom. The state cannot produce community, as Macmurray rightly perceived, but the Church must not arrogate to itself a Christ-like role "to save the world," in Macmurray's unfortunate words, by its own loving existence.[21] Because of our serious situation as sinners, Karl Barth warns, we must be wary of the pride of self-help and all attempts to regain our freedom and responsibility; our only hope is the grace of God.[22]

Miroslav Volf argues,

> ... the social vision based on the doctrine of the Trinity should rest primarily on the downward movement in which God, in a sense, comes out of the circularity of divine love in order to take godless humanity into the divine embrace. A soteriology based on the indwelling of the Crucified by the Spirit (Galatians 2.19-20) grounds a social practice modelled on God's passion for the salvation of the world.[23]

---

19 See especially his two-volume *The Form of the Personal: The Self as Agent* (London: Faber, 1957) and *Persons in Relation* (London: Faber, 1961), and his *Search for Reality in Religion* (London: Allen & Unwin, 1965).

20 Harry Guntrip cites his philosophical training with John Macmurray's "personal relations" school of thought as a deep influence on him and of great significance to the "object relations" school of psychotherapy, which modified the drive theory of classical psychoanalysis in a way remarkably similar to Macmurray's emphasis on persons in relation. See Guntrip's *Personality Structure and Human Interaction: The Developing Synthesis of Psycho-Dynamic Therapy* (NY: International Universities, 1961), 19, 124.

21 *Search for Reality*, 76f.

22 Karl Barth, *Church Dogmatics* (Edinburgh: T & T Clark, 1956), eds. G. W. Bromiley & T. F. Torrance, trans. G. W. Bromiley, IV/1, 458, 463ff.

23 "The Trinity and Social Engagement," in *Doctrine of God and Theological Ethics*, 118.

While Volf grounds his social ethic in the trinitarian love of God for the world, his soteriological emphasis which accents the immanent Trinity lacks a basis and ground in the vicarious humanity of Christ or, as Alan Torrance avers, "participation *en Christou*," because "the ethical requirements and obligations of the Covenant . . . are realized and fulfilled *in and through the faithfulness of Christ* on behalf of an alienated humanity which cannot realize them in and for itself." Torrance's ethic is in integral relationship with prayer and worship because our "one single human response to God" is *given* in Christ and best expressed in the gratitude of "eucharistic participation." As Torrance summarizes,

> He took bread (meaning, he took our humanity), gave thanks (offered that life of gratitude which is the true response in our place), broke it (died in and through taking the alienation of humanity to himself), and gave (giving us back our humanity renewed and sanctified in him). Christian ethics denotes nothing less, therefore, than the gift of participating by the Spirit in that exchange, *katallage*. 'Fundamental ethics' concerns and recognizes no other ethical foundation, therefore, than ecclesial participation in Christ, in the New Covenant, in the *eschatos Adam*.[24]

Christians who base their hope for humanity on a paternal state or politicized church, on the one hand, or on abstract, schizoid intellectualizing about doctrine,[25] on the other hand, neglect the foundation of their faith and the reason of their existence qua the body of Christ. The triune God upholds persons in community or fellowship (such as church, family, or friendship), for the personal relations of humanity reflect the very being of God as a communion of persons in free, mutual, loving, and giving relations. The Christian Church must witness to the personal relations of God's own being known to us in Jesus Christ as a theological basis for contemporary social and political discussions. "The church finds its true ministry," as Anderson

---

24 Alan Torrance, "On Deriving 'Ought' from 'Is': Christology, Covenant and *Koinonia*," 174-5.

25 Cf. Walker Percy, *The Moviegoer* (NY: Ivy, 1960): "The proofs of God's existence may have been true for all I know, but it didn't make the slightest difference. . . . REMEMBER TOMORROW: Starting point for search: It no longer avails to start with creatures and prove God. Yet it is impossible to rule God out. The only possible starting point: the strange fact of one's own invincible apathy — that if the proofs were proved and God presented himself, nothing would be changed. Here is the strangest fact of all. Abraham saw signs and believed. Now the only sign is that all the signs in the world make no difference. Is this God's ironic revenge? But I am onto him" (128f.).

The Humanity of God and the Healing of Humanity

puts it well, "in the upholding, healing and transformation of the humanity of others as already grasped and reconciled to God through the humanity and ministry of Jesus Christ."[26]

What are some concrete implications of this trinitarian-incarnational theology of Christian community in society? Current discussions of "diversity," first of all, tend to run amok of a trinitarian theology of differentiation within unity by emphasizing otherness over oneness. Instead of dynamically balancing the unity and plurality of various peoples in a way that indirectly mirrors the mutual relations of the Trinity, slogans of diversity in schools and society often foster a balkanized society of competing victim groups. Rights replace responsibility; diversity degenerates into divisiveness.

The current emphasis on "diversity" also tends to betray the original civil rights vision of treating all people with individual respect and dignity and not merely as members of a group, or of not discriminating against individuals based on their race, sex, etc. "Affirmative action" programs today treat individuals in precisely the opposite way: as members of groups and not as individuals; some "diversity" programs even attempt to achieve proportional representation of races based on the assumption that "numerical imbalances" indicate a pattern of "institutional racism." This return to a pre-civil rights posture of treating people differently based on race, sex, etc., both patronizes already well-to-do minorities, so that the advantaged benefit in the name of the disadvantaged, and prevents society from moving beyond "white guilt" and "black victimization."[27]

A one-sided emphasis on diversity, often conceived as the color of one's skin (not the content of one's character), tends to promote self-segregating patterns of intolerance and, ironically, uniformity.[28]

---

26 Ray S. Anderson, "Christopraxis: the Ministry and the Humanity of Christ for the World." in *Christ in our Place: The Humanity of God in Christ for the Reconciliation of the World* (Essays presented to Professor James Torrance), ed. Trevor Hart & Daniel Thimell (Eugene, OR: Pickwick), 19ff.

27 See Shelby Steele, *The Content of Our Character: A New Vision of Race in America* (NY: HarperPerennial, 1990), 77ff., 144; Stephen L. Carter, *Reflections of an Affirmative Action Baby* (NY: BasicBooks, 1991), 80.

28 Cf. Percy, *Thanatos Syndrome*: "One of life's little mysteries: an old-style Southern white and an old-style Southern black are more at ease talking to each other, even though one may be unjust to each other, than Ted Kennedy talking to Jesse Jackson — who are overly cordial, nervous as cats in their cordiality, and glad to be rid of each other. In the first case — the old-style white and the old-style black — each knows exactly where he stands with the other. Each can handle the other, the first because he is in control, the

The superficiality of assuming that racial diversity ensures intellectual diversity resorts to the rebuilding of stereotypes, not the demolition of racial walls. Treating people as means to an end and not as ends in themselves (a word on behalf of Kant from the school of Karl Barth and T. F. Torrance!) elevates social engineering schemes over truly affirming one's fellow humanity.

Learning and scholarship, as another example, should be envisioned and practiced for the sake of the formation of persons-in-community and not merely as an impersonal process of accumulating and disseminating information. Analogous to parents passing on wisdom for daily living to their children, teachers should also form relationships with students that should impart learning and wisdom, so that students are equipped for life and not merely for tests![29] The novelist Walker Percy's *Love in the Ruins* portrays the character Dr. Thomas More (ironically named for the author of Utopia), who is a psychiatrist that uses an "ontological lapsometer," or a machine to evaluate patients' emotional disturbances.[30] This "utopian" (Gk: *ou* + *topos* = "no place") doctor, who does not like to deal with actual people and their problems, reminds one of professors who prefer isolating themselves in their offices for research and writing over relating to students.

Schools may thus become sanctuaries instead of factories of learning, engaging the passions of one's heart, mind, and soul — worshipping God with one's whole being in the context of formal courses and informal mentoring relationships. For example (and I follow the lead here of my own mentor, Ray Anderson), I met with small groups of students during lunch time to discuss great works of theology, philosophy, literature, psychology, and so on, which we read prior to such meetings. Our goals were the same as for my formal courses:

---

second because he uses his wits. They both know this and can even enjoy each other. In the second case — Ted Kennedy and Jesse Jackson — each is walking on eggshells. What to say next in this rarified atmosphere of perfect liberal agreement?" (37f.).

29 Will Barrett, the protagonist of Walker Percy's *The Last Gentleman*, is a drifter and searcher, whose education did not prepare him for the reality of life: "The old spurious hope and elegance of school days came back to him. How strange it was that school had nothing whatever to do with life. The old talk of school as a preparation for life — what a bad joke. There was no relation at all. School made matters worse. The elegance and order of school had disarmed him for what came later" (157).

30 "Only in man does the self miss itself, fall from itself (hence lapsometer)" — *Love in the Ruins* (NY: Ivy, 1971), 31.

(1) to read consistently and well as a basis for sharing one's ideas[31];

(2) to learn to listen to others as well as to speak[32]; and

(3) to test out one's ideas in relationship with others, for one does not need to know everything to say something.[33]

Teaching is a personal, social, and spiritual activity, not simply a matter of technique, for it occurs within a context of whole persons in relationship to other whole persons and before the God of Jesus Christ.

Abortion, as a further example, concerns persons in relation: the mother and father, medical personnel, relatives or friends, and society whose attitudes and laws may permit abortion. Centrally, the unborn child too, who in Karl Barth's words, "is a man and not a thing, nor a mere part of the mother's body . . . a fellow-man whose life is given by God . . ." Barth continues by developing a distinctively Protestant theology regarding abortion based on the Gospel: not by underbidding "the severity of the Roman Catholic No" but by replacing its "abstract and negative 'Thou shalt not'" with its own "Thou mayest" — a gracious permission to live life that includes a corresponding obligation to uphold it, and a profound sense of the mystery and awe of life that lives by the freedom of "may" instead of the burden of "must." Barth concludes by noting the need for exceptions, based on the *ultimo ratio* of a pregnant mother's life in jeopardy, done with a clear conscience "before God and in responsibility to Him," and assured "in faith that God will forgive the elements of sin involved."[34]

---

31 "Perhaps the secret of talking was to have something to say," as Walker Percy puts it in *The Second Coming* (NY: Washington Square, 1980), 48.

32 As Karl Barth comments in his *Church Dogmatics*, "Two monologues do not constitute a dialogue" (Edinburgh: T & T Clark, 1960), trans. Harold Knight et al., III/2, 259.

33 As Lessing remarks, "If God held all truth in his right hand, and in his left hand the lifelong pursuit of it, he would choose the left hand" (quoted in *A Kierkegaard Anthology* [Princeton: Princeton Univ., 1973], ed. Robert Bretall, 195). A more accurate but less quotable version appears in *Concluding Unscientific Postscript to Philosophical Fragments* (Princeton: Princeton, 1992), ed. & trans. Howard & Edna Hong: "If God held all truth enclosed in his right hand, and in his left hand the one and only ever-striving drive for truth, even with the corollary of erring forever and ever, and, if he were to say to me: Choose! — I would humbly fall down to him at his left hand and say: Father, give! Pure truth is indeed only for you alone!" (Vol. I, 106).

34 *Church Dogmatics* (Edinburgh: T & T Clark, 1961), trans. A. T. Mackay et al., III/4, 415ff.

To engage in abstract, hypothetical, and technical questions about whether the fetus is human, declares Dietrich Bonhoeffer, merely confuses the issue. "The simple fact," continues Bonhoeffer, "is that God certainly intended to create human life and that this nascent human being has been deliberately deprived of his life."[35] T. F. Torrance also understands the unborn child as "not a potential, but an incipient person"; "an integrated whole"; "genetically complete in the embryo from the moment of conception"; and open "beyond mere empirical observation" to "a regulating force" beyond itself. Such a "dynamic and ontological" relation, an "onto-relational and interrelational way of thinking," understands the unborn child in relation to God himself. God "is the Creative Source of all personal being and inter-personal relations — he is the personalising Person, who brings us into personal life and being through the inter-personal activity of a father and mother" from conception through birth, childhood, and the love of personal family life.[36]

With this theology of abortion in the back of my mind, my wife, Gail, and I faced a life-and-death decision regarding the impending birth of our daughter. When Gail's water broke at twenty-two weeks of gestation, the doctor gravely informed us that our baby would have a ten-percent chance of living, and on the slim chance that she lived, severe abnormalities were likely. Perhaps such a situation granted us the freedom to abort with a clear conscience, at least based on consequentialist calculations and certainly with the announced blessing of our doctor. Perhaps Barth, Torrance, and especially Bonhoeffer (who permits no exceptions) were too severe in not showing openness to God's concrete command in borderline medical situations. Life, after all, is not an absolute right, and our daughter was appearing on the very margins of life.

The fact that our daughter, Jessa, was born alive — albeit at about one pound (16 ozs. at birth and dropping to 13 ozs.), and required critical care for five months and multiple surgeries before gaining relatively normal health — does not justify in retrospect our decision not to abort; this case could have turned out much more grim. Our experience does illustrate, however, the profound and wrenching human decisions that humans must

---

35 Dietrich Bonhoeffer, *Ethics* (NY: Macmillan, 1955), 175f. Also cf. Walker Percy's *Thanatos Syndrome*, which discusses "Doe v. Dude, the landmark case decided by the US. Supreme Court which decreed, with solid scientific evidence, that the human does not achieve personhood until eighteen months" (361)!

36 Thomas F. Torrance, *The Soul and Person of the Unborn Child* (Edinburgh: Handsel, 1999), 8ff.

make in response to God, the author of life, and in community with others of good character and sound judgment.[37] Life is a gift for which we are responsible to uphold before God with a sense of gratitude and awe for the mystery of life.

The celebration of Holy Communion provides a final example of human relations before the God of Jesus Christ. This Sacrament should proclaim week after week the reality and presence of Christ's one body broken for us as a call to the reconciliation of the divisions that continue to plague the Church and the world (denominational, racial, economic, sexual, and so on). Can the Church conscientiously confess belief in "one holy catholic and apostolic Church" (as in the Nicene Creed) and practice "closed communion" — barring fellow Christians and non-Christians, both in need of Christ, because they do not share one's creedal or denominational affiliation? Can the Church truly be and become a place of belonging and community for sinners as a haven in a heartless world?

Christ's community, Barth proclaims,

> points beyond itself. At bottom it can never consider its own security, let alone its appearance. As His community it is always free from itself. In its deepest and most proper tendency it is not churchly, but worldly — the Church with open doors and great windows, behind which it does better not to close itself in upon itself again by putting in pious stained-glass windows. It is holy in its openness to the street and even the alley, in its turning to the profanity of all human life — the holiness which, according to Rom. 12:5, does not scorn to rejoice with them that do rejoice and to weep with them that weep. Its ministry is not additional to its being. It is, as it is sent and active in its mission."[38]

Ray Anderson proclaims in quintessential fashion, "Only the church that is willing to repent of being the church can truly be the church of Jesus Christ."[39] Consider, for example, the many lonely, depressed, anxious,

---

37 Whereas one physician recommended an abortion based on calculations and odds, another physician simply and helpfully announced, "This baby has a real chance!" "The Case of Gail and Her Baby" is published in my *From Conduct to Character*, 21ff. Our story also appeared in The Knoxville News-Sentinel in the "Health 6: Science" section on March 14, 1994.

38 Barth, *Church Dogmatics*, trans. G. W. Bromiley, IV/1, 725.

39 Anderson, *Shape of Practical Theology*, 180. Perhaps Ray would appreciate Walker Percy's characterization of the non-repentant Christian: "I stopped eating Christ in communion, stopped going to mass, and have since fallen into a disorderly life. I

and aimless individuals who attend church week after week in search of community and purpose. Churches can, at times, exacerbate their plight through pointless, non-theological sermons, which fail to proclaim week after week that God comes to us in our greatest point of need to affirm, to uphold, and to redeem us for participation in community with God himself in our midst.

The Church must lead the way in society as a place for belonging and believing, submitting to one Christ, practicing the communion of saints and sinners in true incarnational fashion, confessing a catholic creed of essential theology, and proclaiming the apostolic faith. The Church must practice the unity of its existence in Christ, tolerate the diversity of nonessential dogmas, and participate in the very love of God himself as Father, Son, and Spirit, who graciously permits the Christian community a role of witness in society to the union and communion of God.

---

believe in God and the whole business but I love women best, music and science next, whiskey next, God fourth, and my fellowman hardly at all. Generally I do as I please. A man, wrote John, who says he believes in God and does not keep his commandments is a liar. If John is right, then I am a liar. Nevertheless, I still believe" (*Love in the Ruins*, 6). Percy also writes, "Christ should leave us. He is too much with us and I don't like his friends. We have no hope of recovering Christ until Christ leaves us. There is after all something worse than being God-forsaken. It is when God overstays his welcome and takes up with the wrong people" (*Last Gentleman*, 293).

Chapter 6

Theological Anthropology as a Basis for Christian Ethics in the Theology of Ray S. Anderson

Introduction

Ray Sherman Anderson (1925-2009) was a professor of theology who also served as a parish pastor and always insisted that theology and ministry go hand-in-hand. Like Karl Barth, Anderson articulated a theology of and for the church based on God's own ministry of revelation and reconciliation in the world. As professor and pastor, he modeled in his dealings with his students and congregations an incarnational, evangelical passion for the healing of humanity by Jesus Christ, who is both God's self-revelation to us and the reconciliation of our broken humanity to the triune God. His gift for relating suffering and alienated humans to Christ was a recurrent motif throughout his life, ministry, and works.[1]

---

1 See *The Ray S. Anderson Collection*, Todd H. Speidell, General Editor (Eugene, OR: Wipf & Stock), a collection which comprises books by, about, and in honor of Ray Anderson. Christian D. Kettler's *Reading Ray S. Anderson* (Eugene, OR: Wipf & Stock, 2010) deserves special attention as the first full monograph that introduces Ray's theology for the wide audience it deserves, as well as his tribute to Ray Anderson in *Participatio: The Journal of the Thomas F. Torrance Theological Fellowship*, Supp. Vol. 1 (2011): 1-13. Also see Daniel J. Price, "Community in the Life and Theology of Ray Anderson," in Todd Speidell, ed., *On Being Christian . . . and Human: Essays in Celebration of Ray S. Anderson* (Eugene, OR: Wipf & Stock, 2002), 15-33; and in the same volume, Gary W. Deddo, "Resisting Reductionisms: Why We Need Theological Anthropology," 168-93. For a discussion of Ray Anderson's role in the appropriation of Karl Barth for a transformed North American evangelical theology, see John R. Lewis, *Karl Barth in North America: The Influence of Karl Barth in the Making of a New North American Evangelicalism* (Eugene, OR: Wipf & Stock, 2009), 170-184; Phillip R. Thorne, *Evangelicalism and Karl Barth: His Reception and Influence in North American Evangelical Theology* (Allison Park: Pickwick Pub., 1995), 117-23. Ray Anderson's own essay "Evangelical Theology" in David F. Ford, ed, *The Modern Theologians: An*

Over time Anderson grew tired of the abstract doctrine that he had attempted to preach as a young pastor to bewildered parishioners. After a parishioner confronted him about his arid preaching, he began to develop a profoundly Christ-centered theology and learned anew that the church's ministry and mission participated in the triune God's ministry and mission in the world. He completed his PhD in his late 40s at the University of Edinburgh under T. F. Torrance. He began teaching at Westmont in 1972 and then moved to Fuller Theological Seminary in 1976, where he would spend the rest of his career. He wrote extensively and creatively on theological anthropology, practical theology, and theology of ministry. (The pastoral theologian who began his teaching career in middle age wrote twenty-seven books.) He entered into dialogue with social scientists,[2] but he always insisted on the unique saving and healing activity of God in the vicarious humanity of Christ: namely, that Christ lived and died in our place and on our behalf, and he continues his mission in the world by the Spirit on behalf of the Father.[3]

Introduction to Christian Theology in the Twentieth Century, 2nd ed. (Cambridge: Blackwell, 1997), 480-498, illuminates both evangelical theology and Anderson himself, who concludes with a summons for evangelicals to articulate and practice an integrated gospel in contemporary culture based on the particularity of Jesus Christ (494-495).

2 See Anderson, *Christians Who Counsel: The Vocation of Wholistic Therapy* (Eugene, OR: Wipf & Stock, 2010); *On Being Family: A Social Theology of the Family*, co-author Dennis B. Guernsey (Grand Rapids: Eerdmans, 1985); *Something Old, Something New: Marriage and Family Ministry in a Postmodern Culture* (Eugene, OR: Wipf & Stock, 2007); and the special issue devoted to Ray Anderson, in Todd Speidell, Guest Editor, *Edification: Journal of the Society for Christian Psychology* 1, no. 2 (Eugene, OR: Wipf & Stock, 2007). Also see Anderson's "The Social Ecology of Human Personhood: Implications of Dietrich Bonhoeffer's Theology for Psychology," in Todd Speidell, ed., *On Being a Person*, 146-73; and in this same volume, Anderson's sermon "On Being Christian," in which he observes: "Note that it is not 'on being *a* Christian.' That's an entirely different matter; I'm not sure I'd have a sermon on that. As I read the New Testament literature, I find very little concern for that question: 'on being *a* Christian.' The emphasis is upon being Christian. If you want to know if I am a Christian, you can ask me and I will tell you. I have a testimony to give you that I am a Christian. If you want to know if I am being Christian, you ask my faculty colleagues, and my students, and the people that live and work with me" (255).

3 For an introduction to the vicarious humanity of Christ, see Christian D. Kettler's *The Vicarious Humanity of Christ and the Reality of Salvation* (Lanham: University Press of America, 1991), and especially see Kettler's two volumes that constructively develop this doctrine based on Ray Anderson's mentors, T. F. and J. B. Torrance, *The God Who Believes: Faith, Doubt, and the Vicarious Humanity of Christ* (Eugene, OR: Cascade, 2005), and *The God Who Rejoices: Joy, Despair, and the Vicarious Humanity of Christ* (Eugene. OR: Cascade. 2010).

Anderson did not write a theology of culture. In fact, he commented that H. Richard Niebuhr's classic work *Christ and Culture* "misses the mark." "The critical issue," Anderson avers, "is not how Christ relates to culture but how Christ relates to humanity in every culture."[4] Anderson's doctrine of humanity and love of human beings offered a unique perspective on issues that Christians face in contemporary culture. He emphasized that "the absolute nature of God's truth is grounded in God's Word as a living and active reality rather than in abstract principles or doctrines." At the same time, God's word does not succumb to a pragmatic approach that capitulates "to a convenient expediency. Conformity to the authority of God's Word may require nonconformity to a theological tradition as well as nonconformity to contemporary culture and ideology."[5]

Anderson based his theological anthropology on his many years as a pastoral theologian who dealt with scores of students of all races and nationalities and as a pastor who served suburban congregations in Southern California. He practiced an incarnational and sacramental ministry that attracted all sorts of people, whoever they were or whatever their situation, re-presenting the Christ who ate and drank with sinners and outcasts. Anderson's unity of revealed and reconciled truth in Jesus Christ pointed to God's work in healing our broken humanity.[6] This essay will utilize the case study approach; for, at heart, Professor Anderson was Pastor Anderson and focused his theology on people in need of the love and grace of God.

---

4 Ray S. Anderson, *An Emergent Church Theology for Emerging Churches* (Downers Grove, IL: InterVarsity Press, 2006), 58, n. 12.

5 Ray S. Anderson, *The Soul of Ministry: Forming Leaders for God's People* (Louisville, KY: John Knox Press, 1997), 23-24.

6 Anderson quotes J. B. Torrance: "Christ does not heal us by standing over against us, diagnosing our sickness, prescribing medicine for us to take, and then going away, to leave us to get better by obeying his instructions — as an ordinary doctor might. No, He becomes the patient! He assumes that very humanity which is in need of redemption, and by being anointed by the Spirit in our humanity, by a life of perfect obedience, by dying and rising again, for us, our humanity is healed in him. We are not just healed 'through Christ' because of the work of Christ but 'in and through Christ.'" Ray S. Anderson, "Christopraxis: the Ministry and Humanity of Christ for the World," in *Christ in Our Place: The Humanity of God in Christ for the Reconciliation of the World* (Essays Presented to James B. Torrance), ed. Trevor Hart and Daniel Thimell (Exeter, U.K.: Paternoster Press, 1989), 12.

Fully Human

The Case of Joe

Joe was smart, good, and evangelical. He had excelled at every level, graduating *summa cum laude* from an elite college prep school, distinguishing himself in college and business school, and succeeding in business. He was happily married to Karen, with whom he had three kids, lived in an exclusive neighborhood, and served as a deacon at his church. Despite outward appearances Joe had a hidden problem: he drank. He started as a young kid, which was especially risky given his family history of alcoholism, but he convinced himself that he was just having fun and relieving the stress of school and family. When he went to college, he drank heavily, especially on weekends or occasional weeknights when his friends wanted to go out and get away from the tedium of academia.[7]

After he began his family and career, he continued to drink but concealed his behavior from most of his family and friends. His drinking buddies agreed with him that the stress of success warranted relief by the common and socially acceptable use of alcohol. "Everyone drinks," one friend reassured him, "and as long as you don't become an alcoholic, it's not a big deal." Karen observed his tendency to rely on alcohol, especially under times of stress, but she thought he had it under control because he managed his life so well. Joe had attended counseling sessions with Ray for his dependency upon alcohol, although Joe did not consider himself an "alcoholic." He attended Alcoholics Anonymous (AA) meetings, but did not identify with attendees whose lives were out of control compared to his.

Joe had too many beers one Sunday afternoon while watching a game on television. While preparing to enter church for the evening service, he saw Pastor Ray in the parking lot. Joe spontaneously disclosed to Ray that he was very sorry he could not attend church. "Pastor," he confessed with shame, "I cannot attend church in good conscience, but may we meet on Wednesday to talk? I will attend extra AA meetings during the week and hope I can be back on track so I can worship God in a worthy manner."

"Joe," Pastor Ray said with confidence, "your church community is precisely where you need to be at this moment. Join the rest of us as we

---

7 The Case of Joe appears in Anderson's *The Soul of Ministry*, 166-75; ch. 19: "The Ministry of the Church as a Sacrament of Forgiveness and Healing." I have assumed the liberty of amending and amplifying this case to encompass others' similar stories from my personal and pastoral experience to illustrate key themes in Ray Anderson's pastoral theology. Names or identifying details associated with the case have been changed.

all come in need to meet Jesus in his saving and healing presence as and through the church. We can talk later about alcohol, but right now you especially need your Savior." While Joe's somewhat inebriated appearance and odor in church caused some in the congregation to protest, Pastor Ray upheld his conviction that Christ is the primary Sacrament who came to heal the very humanity he assumed.

On Being Human

Anderson's theological anthropology dares to begin with humanity because Christ has assumed and healed our fallen humanity. He disagrees with "the caricature of Barth's theology as hopelessly constricted by christological and eschatological concerns, and thus left with no place for authentic human existence. . . . Because Barth takes the humanity of Jesus Christ with absolute seriousness, he takes the concrete and creaturely humanity of all persons seriously." Anderson claims the only basis for theological anthropology is the very humanity of Jesus Christ.[8]

---

8 Ray S. Anderson, *On Being Human: Essays in Theological Anthropology* (Grand Rapids: Eerdmans, 1982), viii. Anderson agrees with Barth's critical qualification: "There is a way from Christology to anthropology, but there is no way from anthropology to Christology," from *Church Dogmatics*, I/1, ed. G. W. Bromiley & T. F. Torrance (Edinburgh: T & T Clark, 1975), 131. Anderson says he follows Karl Barth's dictum: "theology has become anthropology since God became man" (ibid., viii), which has no citation and appears to be a misquotation from Karl Barth's *Protestant Theology in the Nineteenth Century*, which I will quote in context: "'Theology has long since become anthropology' — from the moment when Protestantism itself, and Luther in particular, ceased to be interested in what God is in himself and became emphatically interested in what God is for man. Theology's course of development has irresistibly proceeded in such a way that man has come more and more to renounce God, in proportion as he has come to proclaim himself. And it is an open secret that Christianity in its theological form has long since disappeared, not only from the sphere of reason, but also from the actual life of mankind; and that man's awakened self-consciousness has meant that Christianity in this form is no longer taken seriously. Religion exists. Religion is possible and necessary. But it is man who is the beginning, the middle and the end of religion — man and man alone." Barth's concern for objective thinking about God, which Anderson follows as a student of T. F. Torrance, militates against Feuerbach's reduction of theology to anthropology, which is reflected in his quotation from Feuerbach's *The Essence of Christianity* (above). Barth concludes his critique of Feuerbach by noting that his conflation of knowledge of God with knowledge of ourselves has misunderstood both God and humanity: "Like all the theologians of his time, Feuerbach discussed man in general, and in attributing divinity to him in his sense had in fact not said anything about man as he is in reality"! (Valley Forge: Judson, 1973), 536, 539.

Anderson quotes Barth to explain the premise of his theological anthropology:

> Thus the fact that I am born and die, that I eat and drink and sleep, that I develop and maintain myself; that beyond this I assert myself in the face of others, and even physically, propagate my species; that I enjoy and work and play in fashion and possess; that I acquire and have and exercise powers; that I take part in all the work of the race, either accomplished or in process of accomplishment; that in all this, I satisfy religious needs and can realize religious possibilities; and that in it all I fulfill my aptitudes as an understanding and thinking, willing and feeling being — all this as such is not my humanity. In it all I must first answer the question, whether I will affirm or deny my humanity. It is only the field on which human being either takes place or does not take place as history, as the encounter of the I and Thou; the field on which it is revealed or obscured that "I am as Thou art." That I exist on this field, and do so in a particular way, does not of itself mean that I am human.[9]

Humanity is more basic than religion, churches (and H. Richard Niebuhr!) take note. A non-theological anthropology, whether religious or not, errs by substituting the disordered human person as the focus and center of what it means to be human, rather than Jesus Christ as the true and archetypal form of humanity. Anderson observes, "It is not because a non-theological anthropology lacks a kerygma that it is non-theological, but because the kerygma by which it purports to give meaning to personal human existence is a pseudo-kerygma. It is a 'word' which has been conceived in silence and fabricated out of desperate longings and lonely desperation." He quotes Barth, "in the last resort there is something tragic in every non-theological anthropology."[10]

---

9 Quoted in *On Being Human*, 21-22.

10 *On Being Human*, 10, 14 (see 8-19 for a discussion of theological vs. non-theological anthropology). Consider, for example, Larry David (co-creator and writer of Seinfeld) in Woody Allen's *Whatever Works* (2009) at a New Year's party pathetically pontificating on "meaningless blind chance": "I happen to hate New Year's celebrations. Everybody desperate to have fun, trying to celebrate in some pathetic little way. Celebrate what? A step closer to the grave?... Whatever love... happiness... temporary measure of grace. Whatever works. Don't kid yourself... A bigger part of your existence is luck than you like to admit." I have analyzed the implicit theology of Woody Allen's pseudo-kerygma more fully in my "God, Woody Allen, and Job" essay in *Christian Scholar's Review* 29, no. 3 (2000): 551-61, which is reprinted here as Appendix B.

Anderson argues for a contingent relationship between creaturely (sixth day) and personal (seventh day) existence that a non-theological anthropology merely conflates. Of all the sixth day creatures, God summons only human beings for fellowship with himself on the seventh day. Hence the seventh day serves as an eschatological orientation and priority for the sixth day, which has chronological precedence but no inherent teleological determination. For creation presupposes the covenant God and nature presupposes grace. Hence, the eschatological priority of seventh day orientation for sixth day existence distinguishes a theological from a non-theological anthropology. Thus, treating human beings as mere creatures depersonalizes them.[11] Anderson writes,

> "If there is any basis for social justice, it lies between us, within our humanity; it is anthropological.... Social justice is a human, not merely an ethical, problem.... The vicarious humanity of Christ binds both the victim and the oppressor to God. But even more, the continuing humanity of God in Christ binds God to the cause of social justice from the side of those who suffer injustice."[12]

Ethical issues, then, must be decided on the field of humanity, for the critical issues of life are "fundamentally anthropological." The process of dying, for example, is not merely a sixth day phenomenon, for "it is irresponsible to surrender the determination of the dignity of a human person to a biological and technological process." One has an "inescapable responsibility of acting humanly before God in certain critical situations" with fear and trembling, "for the absolute certainty that one is right is perilously close to being wrong (cf. Jn 9:16)." The Christian community has a responsibility to uphold human beings at the margins of life.[13]

---

11 *On Being Human*, 23-26, 65; also see *The Soul of Ministry*, 52-59.

12 Anderson, *The Shape of Practical Theology: Empowering Ministry with Theological Praxis* (Downers Grove, IL: InterVarsity Press, 2011), 312-13, from ch. 19, "The Little Man on the Cross: Where is God When We Suffer?" Other chapters cover a variety of issues, including the risen Lord as the "hermeneutical criterion" for parity between men and women in ministry, the church's presence in the city, homosexuality, and other sociocultural implications of Christian ethics and pastoral care based on a Christian theological anthropology.

13 *On Being Human*, 151-58. Anderson objects to Stanley Hauerwas' willingness to give up the grammar of personhood. He suggests an alternative title to Hauerwas' essay, "My Uncle Charlie Is Not Much of a Person But He Is Still My Uncle Charlie": "Every Patient is a Person, and My Uncle Charlie is a Person Too!" in his response essay, "The Ground and Grammar of Personhood," *Journal of Religion, Disability, and Health* 8, no. 3 (2004): 121-25.

The "wholeness of personhood is the responsibility of the community, and not merely the responsibility of the self." For Christian community reenacts the healing ministry of Christ himself, whose ongoing ministry and humanity continue as "the ontological grounding of the church as the people of God." This community is the place where the Spirit of Christ joins and unites sinners to God's own fellowship of being as Father, Son, and Spirit. The liturgical events of Christian community exist to reaffirm, support, and heal those who gather in need.[14]

Anderson views the Lord's Supper as an event of belonging to Christ, even and especially for those who do not believe. Paul's warning to the Corinthians did not address unbelievers but believers, especially those who excluded those in need. Jesus' ministry was characterized by his communion with and ministry to sinners and outcasts; people like Joe.[15] "Wherever humanity finds itself," Anderson announces, "no matter how tattered and torn, no matter how lost and forlorn, is where liturgical acts should take place. For here there is vulnerability, here it counts."[16]

Chris Kettler rightly notes that, in Anderson's trinitarian-incarnational theology, Christ communed with publicans and sinners before he created the church. "At the heart of a trinitarian-incarnational theology," Kettler proclaims, "is the real presence of Christ." Christ's sacramental ministry and mission often occurred in the midst of mundane places and activities, such as eating and drinking with sinners and outcasts. Christ's "relational" ministry was no mere evangelistic technique to make the gospel "relevant" to contemporary culture. Rather, it more deeply reflected the very relationship between the Father and the Son in the Spirit. "What (Anderson) proposes," Kettler observes, "is to reconcile the chasm between the doctrine of God and the doctrine

---

14 *On Being Human*, 182-86.

15 *The Soul of Ministry*, 170-71.

16 *On Being Human*, 189-91. Anderson quotes Michael Polanyi to support his view of the social nature of humanity: "Our believing is conditioned at its source by our belonging." He also quotes John Macmurray, "I need you to be myself. This need is for a fully positive personal relation in which, because we trust one another, we can think and feel and act together. Only in such a relation can we really be ourselves . . . For what we really need is to care for another, and we are only caring for ourselves. We have achieved society, but not community. We have become associates, but not friends" (see *On Being Human*, quoted on 169-70; also see Kettler, *Reading Ray S. Anderson*, "The Lord's Supper as Doing Evangelism and Sustaining Personhood," 105-8).

of the church, two doctrines that have historically rarely spoken to one another!"[17]

The incarnation bridges the gap. "Because of the incarnation," Kettler comments, "the humanity God took upon himself was the totality of our humanity, not just our 'spirituality.'"[18] God's gracious intervention in our human alienation creates faith and joy from God's side amidst our doubt and despair. "The vicarious humanity of Christ," he counsels, "claims that all of our responses should be based on the human response of Christ," which does not mean "all of grace" and "nothing of our humanity in it." It is precisely the opposite: "The Son's 'Amen' to the Father is an eternal amen that is now said in our humanity as a gift of grace."[19] "Christ taking our place," Kettler observes, "does not mean that we are no longer in the picture. Rather *a genuine understanding of substitutionary atonement includes our union with Christ*. Even Barth, with his concern for the transcendence and grace of God will admit that 'It is a poor theology that persists in the inequality between me and Jesus Christ — a pious cushion which is content to maintain the distinction from Him.'"[20]

---

17 See Kettler, *Reading Ray S. Anderson*, 124. Anderson's emphasis on "Living in the World" evidenced itself early in his career as a chapter of his dissertation was published as *Historical Transcendence and the Reality of God* (Grand Rapids: Eerdmans, 1975). It was later reprinted in his edited volume *Theological Foundations for Ministry* (Edinburgh: T & T Clark, 1979), 567-94. Anderson's introductory essay, "A Theology for Ministry," in the latter work also served as an early signal of his trinitarian-incarnational theology for ministry and mission.

18 Christian D. Kettler, *The God Who Believes: Faith, Doubt, and the Vicarious Humanity of Christ* (Eugene, OR: Cascade, 2005), 11.

19 Christian D. Kettler, *The God Who Rejoices: Joy, Despair, and the Vicarious Humanity of Christ* (Eugene, OR: Cascade, 2010), 185. Kettler writes in dialogue with Barth, "To be created is cause for gratitude before the Creator. Despite the potential for despair, how could it be otherwise? The command of God, Barth argues, is not be received without joy. 'One cannot be obedient to God's command without both joy and seriousness.' In fact, Barth is bold enough to say, 'The will for life is also the will for joy.' The most solemn and serious person cannot deny this. Joy, therefore, should not be dismissed as naïve and childish but can even be seen at the center of Christian ethics: 'And the question what it means to will to be happy in obedience is in its place just as serious, and its correct answering is just as important and as little self-evident, as any ethical question'" (ibid., 179). "Barth can even speak of a 'readiness for joy' that comes from acknowledging life as God's gift of grace" (ibid., 223).

20 Ibid., 276f. Emphasis added to underscore that my emphasis on participation in Christ as the proper ground of a Christian ethic must occur in union with Christ for an active, filial, and evangelical social ethic.

Fully Human

Jesus Christ, Anderson believes, is fully God and truly human, so that we find our true humanity in him. Christ continues to meet us in our human need through the church community, not through "religious or pseudo-religious privatism." In Anderson's words:

> The church becomes the specific and concrete occasion for experiencing, even if imperfectly, the true order of existence in fellowship. Belonging to this fellowship is not the prerogative of the healthy minded or the privileged or the successful. It is Christ himself who stands as the Lord of the church with his words of reminder, 'Those who are well have no need of a physician but those who are sick.' The true order of the church thus includes the cure of souls, and must therefore include those in need of cure.[21]

The cure of souls should not become "a superfluous religious duplication" of secular service (reducing pastoral counsel to social work) nor a separate "religious" sphere (divorcing church worship from human need) but a distinctive service of Jesus Christ. Anderson agrees with Dietrich Bonhoeffer, "The religious person divides life into sectors, of which religion accounts for only one, rather than encompassing the entirety of human existence, as he himself believed the incarnation demanded."[22] As T. F. Torrance kerygmatically insists:

> The Church cannot be in Christ without being in Him as He is proclaimed to men in their need and without being in Him as He encounters us in and behind the existence of every man in his need. Nor can the Church be recognized as His except in that meeting of Christ clothed with His Gospel in the depth of human misery, where Christ clothed with His Gospel meets with Christ clothed with the desperate need and plight of men.[23]

The church must avoid the dual temptation of "either 'playing God' with presumed omnipotence or copping out altogether and resorting to caring as a substitute for curing." The church must "dare to grasp what is out of order for the sake of orienting it to the true order": relating those who are in pain and suffering to the actual healing of humanity in Christ, which

---

21 *On Being Human*, 199, 202.

22 *On Being Human*, 195-8.

23 T. F. Torrance, "Service in Jesus Christ," in *Theological Foundations for Ministry: Selected Readings for a Theology of the Church in Ministry*, ed. Ray S. Anderson (Grand Rapids: Eerdmans, 1979), 724.

we may experience both provisionally and finally.[24] The church can offer nothing less than Jesus Christ himself to those in need, especially for those on the margins of church life and community.

The Case of Joe (resumed)

After years of quiet but heavy drinking, Joe started going to bars with his drinking buddies after work every day and isolating himself from his friends and family during a year-long binge, even while continuing to attend church. One day, he finally collapsed, and his wife, Karyn, called 911. She also called Pastor Ray and her Al-Anon sponsor, Joann, to meet them at the hospital. The medical staff had Joe on a ventilator and said that the veins from his liver to his stomach were weak and giving way. They could not save his life. Pastor Ray sat with Karen, listened to her, and talked with her during the protracted treatment. A doctor finally appeared and asked Karen whether she wanted them to continue the extraordinary measures to keep him alive. She did not understand the question: Of course she wanted Joe to live, but why would she authorize continued artificial breathing and blood transfusions that would prove futile?

She asked the doctor for a moment and talked with Pastor Ray. After listening to her acknowledge that Joe's life was over, Pastor Ray gently suggested it was time to let him "die in Christ," to rely on his being in the faithful hands of God, not on the artificial continuation of his biological existence. She soon informed the doctor that she was ready to let go of her husband, and Pastor Ray affirmed her decision to entrust the person Joe, whom she knew and loved, to God.[25]

Ray invited Karen to attend church on Sunday, but she replied, "I can't understand a God who allows good people to make such bad decisions and die so tragically." "I don't believe in that God," he told her. "When Joe tried to exclude himself from church because of his condition, I implored him to be with Christ as he is present to us in community, and he relented. I wanted for him not to segregate himself from Christian community and opt for AA as a sole alternative. We will gather tomorrow, and I hope you will join us. Being with us is more basic than whether you feel right now

---

24 *On Being Human*, 205-6.

25 See Anderson, *Theology: Death and Dying* (Oxford: Blackwell, 1986), especially 48, 99, 115, 130, 137-38, 143-57; and see his *Spiritual Caregiving as Secular Sacrament: A Practical Theology for Professional Caregivers* (London: Jessica Kingsley, 2003), 163-78.

that you can muster up belief in God in the midst of your loss." "But what about Holy Communion," she questioned, "since I wouldn't want to drink and eat unworthily?" Pastor Ray replied, "St. Paul warned the community not to drink and eat unworthily, not those who felt a sense of not being 'right' before God. As I said to Joe, if we excluded you, or said nothing while you excluded yourself, it is we who should feel a sense of remorse about celebrating communion with Christ, who came for all of us who are in need."

Joe's wife sensed a genuine invitation to belong, even while she struggled to believe. She couldn't add up Joe's life-long problem that led to his death, despite his being a faithful member and elder of their church. She wondered if she should go to church, Al-Anon, or just figure it out on her own, if she could. She longed for help but didn't know where to turn.

Meanwhile, Joanne, her Al-Anon sponsor, arrived and sat next to Pastor Ray, whom she knew because Ray's church sponsored AA and Al-Anon meetings. He remarked how Joe had compartmentalized his life: he went to church, although he never felt a sense of belonging while he drank, and he attempted but abandoned AA in the end to return to his drinking buddies in desperate search of a community. Joanne replied that many alcoholics feel like outsiders, even when they attend church. Bill Wilson, co-founder of AA, also felt divided. She briefly told Ray Bill Wilson's story:

> Bill Wilson was an alcoholic. A good friend of his, Ebby Thacher, visited Bill at the lowest point of his drinking career, and invited him to attend a meeting of a Christian organization, the Oxford Group, which had helped him recover from his own alcoholism. He invited Bill to join him for a worship service run by the Oxford Group. A few weeks later, Bill stumbled in drunk to the worship service, went forward after the altar call, and then stood up to make a profession of faith. Although later he could not recall what he had said, he did remember that people listened attentively to him! A few days later, he checked into a hospital for detoxification, cried out to God for delivery, and experienced a miraculous healing of his obsession to drink.

Recognizing the significant role Ebby had played in his healing, Bill felt the deep conviction to do the same for other suffering alcoholics. He discovered that he had remained sober merely by sharing his own story with them. His first success with another alcoholic came a few months later when he suddenly felt the temptation to drink. Bill knew that he had to reach out to a "drunk" in order to stay sober himself. He encountered Dr. Bob Smith, who himself experienced liberation from his own bondage simply by listening to Bill Wilson's story. They believed something extraordinary had happened to them and set out to create a program of recovery they hoped to bring to all alcoholics.

Right from the start, however, they ran into a dilemma. Bill and Bob believed that Jesus Christ had healed them of their alcoholism, but they wanted to reach as many alcoholics as possible, irrespective of religious faith or doctrine. After discussion with other founding members, they decided upon a compromise position of letting members acknowledge the god of their own understanding.[26] In the following years, Bill continued to seek sources of healing outside of AA, most notably in the place where his own story began — the Christian church. Nevertheless, while he had spent much time in study and in counsel with clergy, Bill did not want to alienate other AA members by joining a church, even though he actively encouraged other members to do so. Yet Bill could not help but ask himself if, despite his best attempts at inclusivity, something vitally important had not been left out.[27]

Ray replied that he found the story tragic, especially the perception that the Lord who healed them did not have a large enough table to commune with sinners and outcasts, including unbelievers. The real God who heals us, including Bill Wilson himself, is no generic god. Bill, Ray observed, was

---

26 *Pass It On: The Story of Bill Wilson and How the A.A. Message Reached the World* (New York: Alcoholics Anonymous World Service, Inc., 1984). "In order to carry the principle of inclusiveness and tolerance still further, we make no religious requirement of anyone. All people having an alcohol problem who wish to get rid of it and make a happy adjustment with circumstances of their lives, become A.A. members by simply associating with us. In this atmosphere, the orthodox, the unorthodox, and the unbeliever mix happily and usefully together, and in nearly every case great spiritual growth ensues" (173). "The result of this was the phrase 'God as we understand Him,' which I don't think ever had much of a negative reaction anywhere" (198).

27 *The Language of the Heart: Bill W's Grapevine Writings* (1988, repr; New York, NY: The AA Grapevine, Inc., 2002). "Surely by the hundreds, and probably by the thousands, our friends in the clergy have since continued to go out on the limb. They install our meetings in their basements and social halls. Never interfering with our affairs, they sit in the back — explaining that they have come to AA to learn. When Sunday arrives, they preach sermons about us. They send us prospects and marvel at their progress. When we sometimes ask them to speak to us, they invariably apologize for their own ineffectiveness with alcoholics. This is humility for sure . . . too much of it, perhaps" (178) ". . . Quite rightly, AA didn't try to answer all of my questions, however important they seemed to me . . ." (178-79). "The fact is that I feel deeply the great power and spirituality which flows out into the world through the church. I know of no other source of like quality" (*Pass It On*, 284).

longing for the church to be the church of Jesus Christ. He suggested that the two of them work together to help Karen receive what Bill and Joe could not: holistic healing that connects the good work of AA and Al-Anon to the God of Jesus Christ, who lives and speaks and heals people in need.

Conclusion

The church must avoid splitting the "spiritual" ministry of the church from "secular" or pseudo-religious service in society, taking only the first as its calling, as if one could compartmentalize one's spiritual from one's personal and social life. Joe found his sacramental community with fellow alcoholics on Saturday night but not among his Christian brothers and sisters on Sunday morning. The body of Christ needs to be the place and presence of Christ's healing ministry so that AA participants can learn the name of their "higher power."[28] Joe's experience of alcoholism and the story of Bill Wilson's search for God have helped illustrate how Ray Anderson's theological anthropology addresses humans in need by calling the church to re-present Christ himself to the outcasts of our day, not merely through its mission outreach but especially when the church gathers to proclaim the Word and celebrate the Sacrament. The church must announce and practice its distinctive kerygma, not leaving those like Joe and Bill and their loved ones relying upon themselves and wondering where to turn. Christ offers his healing presence on Sunday morning and Saturday evening alike.

---

28 *The Soul of Ministry*, 172-73.

Appendix A

A Radio Interview with Todd Speidell on Evangelical Social Ethics

Q: In your book *From Conduct to Character*, you make the comment that there are Western assumptions we bring to the table in discussions about ethics. What do you mean by that?

TS: When we in the West discuss moral issues, there are certain traditions that we don't necessarily know explicitly, but that implicitly affect the way we think about morality. These are traditions based on duty or consequences or virtue, which are really the three main traditions for us. There is also what I would consider a fourth and distinct tradition, which is based on God's covenantal commands to be who he created us to be as human creatures in the context of the world he's created. It's a world that is absolutely dependent on God for its existence, yet which he has granted a relative freedom and order of its own. When we look at moral matters in this way, in terms of being God's human creatures and ultimately his new creations in Christ, it casts a different light on these different ethical traditions in Western society.

Q: Can you give us an example of how thinking this way is different from the way we tend to think of things?

TS: Let me make a theoretical point first.

Q: Sure.

TS: Which is that these three different traditions are normally considered very different — like the difference between an ethic based on duty and an ethic based on consequences. For the first, an ethic of duty, you do what's intrinsically right or wrong; for the second, usually a utilitarian ethic, you look at what will produce or what you think will produce the best outcomes for society at large. Those seem like two different traditions, one that's intrinsically right or wrong, and the other measured extrinsically based on outcomes. But there's been a recent revival of an ethic of virtue, which bases ethical thinking not on the sorts of endless dilemmas that academics like to ponder: for example, if your family's out for a boat ride and you capsize and there aren't enough rations for everyone, what are you going to do? These are kinds of silly, abstract, bizarre, extreme dilemmas that we don't face in our daily lives. The virtue ethics folks say that ethics is not merely a matter of decision-making, but it's a consideration of who we are as persons. Now I think that's a helpful corrective, and I think that when you look at Jesus' teachings in the Sermon on the Mount, that he, too, focuses on the heart, what comes from within, and who you are as a person, not simply behaviors. That was a big part of his problem with the Pharisees, since they were so focused on the outward. But with a perspective based on God and his filial obligations for us as his human creatures, those three usual options in Western society are really different ways of being human-centered — whether it is a question of what I shall do or what kind of person I am— the focus is on the self and not on God and what he expects of us. And that really is the original sin: autonomy, including moral autonomy, which is to say that we want to govern ourselves. An example in Scripture is that first decision of Adam and Eve that, contrary to God's concrete command not to eat of the tree, they considered it good for food. Not that they were doing something that was intrinsically wrong, but they were defying God's concrete command to them and for them, and thus violating their natures as human persons. I'll pause there and let you follow up as you like.

Q: What are the implications, then, if we view God and his commands as objectively outside of ourselves, having a bearing on what we think of as right or wrong?

TS: Well, the implications are multifarious; there are all sorts of implications. From a Christian perspective it's a matter of listening to God and his commands in all of life, so that we may be who we are and are becoming in Christ. A contemporary but secondary example, I think, is posting the Ten Commandments in courthouses. The Ten Commandments are the commandments of the God who has brought the people of Israel—who has brought us! — out of Egypt. The Ten Commandments start with, "I am the LORD, your God, who brought you out of the land of Egypt," and that important preamble cannot be left behind! The commandments are the commands of the God who has been there for us and who has set us free! So it's important for us to witness to that God who has liberated us from slavery, and not merely to uphold his commandments as if the commandments in and of themselves have some great, saving impact on society. That's one example of how we need to appreciate the biblical witness and history as truly objective — and it's an example of how Evangelicals need to be more evangelical!

Q: Then what should be the implications for God's commandments in contemporary American society, especially for evangelicals with a theological conscience?

TS: The implications are that when we obey his commandments, which he requires us to do, we are following the living God. One of the commandments — Thou shalt not commit adultery — is one of my favorite examples of the type of relativism that is pervasive in our society. One of the textbooks that I used to use in Ethics courses (and it was this kind of frustration that led me to write my own book) has pro and con essays on whether one ought to commit adultery. That's absurd. There ought to be some things — even a few things! — that all of us in common can say are absolutes. Adultery, rape, torture, and genocide: there ought to be a short list of moral absolutes that all of us can say are indisputable. They're not up for grabs, and we're not going to debate them. But simply because one doesn't commit adultery does not mean that one has followed what Jesus considered the spirit or deeper and personal meaning of the command. For example, take someone who lusts after someone else, but hasn't technically committed adultery: Jesus said that person has violated the spirit of the command.

Now that higher standard Jesus implements puts us all in a situation that's much tougher, because we not only want to be right regarding outward behavior, but also with respect to the inward, our hearts. But I think the Sermon on the Mount, Jesus' life and ministry, and his teachings, just like the Ten Commandments, should not be abstracted from Jesus himself. The Sermon on the Mount is a call to follow Jesus, not simply a command to follow certain rules.

Q: As a follow-up to that, which comes first, the outward or the inward?

TS: God comes first! We acknowledge God as the one who has created us, who has restored us to who we truly are in Christ, and who as the objective one outside of us and apart from us, he comes first. Now God restores us from within! Jesus came as a human. He took our humanity, our broken humanity, upon himself and healed it. And he gives it back to us through his Spirit, and we are to be who we are and are becoming in him. So in a sense there is a priority of the inward. But that's not based on us, whether our behavior or decisions or character, whether on our own efforts at repentance and renewal, but on the act of God breaking into our history, and restoring us to himself and to one another in Christ.

Q: What's a good example in society today if we take seriously and acknowledge that the inward is basic for the outward, in other words, what is inside of a person is influencing the behavior rather than the other way around?

TS: I think a good example of that is so-called "affirmative action," which from my perspective unintentionally rebuilds the dividing walls that Christ has broken down. In Christ there is neither male nor female, slave nor free: Christ has broken down the dividing walls of hostility between us. Affirmative action sets up new forms of racial stereotyping — and ironically they are based on what is now called "diversity," but what I think is a kind of *uniformity*, where diversity is merely seen as the color of one's skin and membership as part of the group. So affirmative action looks at external things, but the Gospel is concerned about internal things. When Onesimus went back to his master, Philemon, he went back as a brother in the Lord. He went back as a slave — that is the external — but the internal had been so radically turned around that the external was profoundly shaken up to the point where both slave and master must have a new type of relationship based on God changing our very humanity from the inside out. Affirmative action looks primarily at external matters, at the color of our skin and not the content of our character, but the Gospel of Jesus Christ shakes us and transforms us and heals us from the inner depths of our humanity to and throughout all aspects of our lives.

Q: You mentioned earlier when you talked about absolutes, isn't that itself an acknowledgement of an objective God who stands over against us and an assumption that needs to be brought into this discussion?

TS: Yes it is. There's a deep interrelationship between God's own objectivity and the objectivity of morality. The moral order of the universe, no less than the physical, is part of the order which God has created and sustains by his Word. In other words, God has endowed his creation not only with an objective physical order, but with a no less objective moral order. Just as we cannot in good reason deny the laws of the physical order, so we cannot in good conscience disobey the laws of the moral order. Morality is more than a convenient way of arranging our lives for the greatest possible good or happiness. It's as much a part of the created order as gravity or light. That's why it cannot be reduced to the subjective preferences of individuals or cultures. But we need to be careful not to absolutize the moral order, or even God's commands, over God himself! God himself is the absolute. Recurrent throughout the Old Testament is the central theme: "I am your God; you *shall* be my people. That *shall* is a command to us: We are to obey God. But it is also a promise: You *shall* be my people. God who makes us into new persons, into a new people, he is the absolute.

That doesn't mean things like adultery and divorce are merely relative. No. God has created this world in such a way that this could never be no matter how many would like to have it otherwise. We don't have a vote in that matter. But by focusing on God and his commands within the context of the good created order in which he has placed us, we may steer both away from legalism and libertinism. In the Bible the indicative always precedes *and* includes the imperative. "I am your God" (that's the indicative); "In Christ all things are reconciled" (again, the indicative); "I am the Lord your God who brought you out of Egypt" (another indicative) — and the indicatives of grace always follow with God's commands and obligations for who we are as his chosen and redeemed people. The problem with legalism is that it tries to prioritize the imperative, so that we have the imperative without the indicative, the command without the promise, and we end up with legal relations rather than filial relations. The New Testament is very filial: focusing on the Father/Son relationship as the basis for our relationship with Christ.

Q: That was my follow-up question. What bearing does the Incarnation have on this?

TS: Everything. If you read the Old Testament, you see the story of the priority of God, the God who has created us, the God who put us in fellowship with himself and with one another, the God who has provided for us and liberated us. And the other side of that story is disobedient Israel looking after other gods, creating other idols. When we read that story, we need to read it with a mirror to ourselves to see our own disobedience. The New Testament is not a rejection of the Old Testament. Christ comes as the one true Israelite. He comes out of Israel as the true Israelite who brings God to us and reconciles us to God. He takes our humanity upon himself and heals it and gives it back to us that we may be whole. What's more, in Jesus Christ God has not only healed our humanity, but the whole created order. All things, visible and invisible, are reconciled and gathered up in Jesus Christ as their Head and Lord. All things are reconciled in

Christ — the indicative. The imperative: We are to be who we are and are becoming in him and not reinsert disorder into the world by recreating dividing walls of hostility that he has torn down.

Q: Certainly we find ourselves — and I don't mean to politicize human matters — but is it possible to lay your paradigm over against governmental policies, some of the issues being discussed in society today, some of the things that we engage ourselves in regarding social and cultural issues?

TS: I think so. We always have to remember that the church is the church, and it needs to be the church, so it should not become another political institution or lobby group. Having said that, God has reconciled our world so that we do need to think and act politically and favor issues, items, and agendas that approximate our own theological convictions. Dietrich Bonhoeffer in Nazi Germany tried to balance a tension between thinking realistically about human nature on the one hand, never being naïve, and on the other hand thinking theologically of God's action in Christ and how we should thus live in society. Bonhoeffer was a pacifist who followed the Sermon on the Mount quite literally — turn the other cheek — and he thought that there were specific implications for society. But he was also a realist. He knew that he could not sit back idly and naïvely while Jews were being killed in his name, because as a German citizen his friends and neighbors were being killed in his name. So we need to act responsibly in society. Often times there isn't a clear right or wrong, but we do the best to approximate our convictions, and Bonhoeffer thought we need to ask for forgiveness and we need to be careful not to justify whatever we choose to do. For example, with Bonhoeffer, he joined the conspiracy against Hitler's life, but he never attempted to justify that action because in the real world you sometimes have to make compromises, and if you're simply utilitarian, one of the Western ethical traditions I mentioned, you can say, well, to kill one to save 6 million, that's an easy calculation. But for Bonhoeffer, who had his own version of a biblical pacifism, he took "Thou shalt not kill" quite seriously and literally, and yet he still felt a need to act responsibly. Now that was in a situation in which he was acting in response to violence and genocide. Preemptive war, as we've witnessed in recent years, is a whole other matter. There is rarely a unanimous opinion anywhere, including in the Christian church, but from pacifists to just war theorists alike, preemptive war is not an option. War is a last resort; it's in defense. Conservatives in particular should speak out against preemptive

Appendix A

war based on our view of sinful human nature and its consequent view of the limits of government, both nationally or internationally.

Q: Is it possible for the church to confuse Christian social responsibility with mere political activity?

TS: Yes, you see that on the Right and on the Left where the church becomes just another political action group. It fixates on certain issues. I have convictions about a variety of issues, but I hope the church never becomes merely another social service agency, another political lobby group, because when it does that it has failed its own mission and it has ceased to heed our Lord for our own agendas. So that is a big concern: the church needs to balance a fine tension between quietism and activism.

Q: What's the key for Christians to think clearly about these issues?

TS: Reading through the biblical story, God has acted in our lives, God has spoken to us, God has restored us. Christ has both revealed God to us and reconciled us to God and to one another. I like to keep that paradigm in mind as I think about different issues — for example, abortion is a big issue. When I think about that profoundly personal matter from my own paradigm, I want to acknowledge God as the Creator of humanity, and Christ through his Spirit as the redeemer of humanity, so it's important to uphold the humanity of the unborn child. This is not just my unborn child: this is a child of God, especially over and against the view of abortion as a legal right, as a matter of personal convenience, or as a way of dealing with the so-called *unwanted child* — such horrible language!

Of course, there are extreme exceptions which should remain extreme, like the life of the mom. This is something we had to deal with in my family. It started before my wife was even pregnant. She was 35 at the time, and her doctor said when she became pregnant that she should consider prenatal testing to evaluate the status and health of the fetus. At the time the very testing that was being recommended had predictable outcomes that could maim or even kill the unborn child, and yet the tests were strongly recommended and almost forced upon us without discussion, and they really had no other purpose than to consider an abortion or a very weak rationale of "emotional preparedness" for a Downs' baby. As it turned out, at only 22 weeks my wife's water broke, which is such a critical period because it was on the borderline time of viability for our unborn child. So we saw a doctor in an emergency situation, and practically the first words out of his mouth were to recommend an abortion, which we decided against.

Two weeks later, having fought against the odds of an imminent and extremely premature childbirth, with all of its possible outcomes and problems, our baby went into cardiac distress and the doctor recommended against an emergency C-section. Now an emergency C-section maximized the best chance of survival for our child, but it did raise certain health concerns for the mom because it's still early enough in the pregnancy that there could be serious, even if remote, repercussions for the mom. So this doctor, and we'd been in conversation with him for a couple of weeks, inundated us with calculations and odds about problems, etc., and even during this critical time he continued with those kind of consequentiality calculations. Another doctor, a Roman Catholic woman, simply walked in and said, "This baby has a real chance."

She cut through all of the calculating consequences, which again is a kind of implicit ethical tradition where you focus on the outcomes, what could happen, all the possible outcomes, etc. This other physician simply said, "This baby has a real chance."

And then my wife had the emergency C-section, and we were fortunate and grateful to have a healthy girl, even though we were prepared for worse. There was no guarantee of what would happen, but in our society there are all sorts of implicit assumptions about ethical models that we operate with, but we were fortunate to have a doctor who walked in and simply announced: "This baby has a real and clear chance."

Q: Is there anything else you want to add?

TS: I think I've said my basic point. I guess the main thing I wanted to focus on is just that the church's role in society is to announce and embody the reconciling presence and ministry of Christ. He has come to break down barriers: barriers between us and God and barriers between us and others, whether male and female, Jew and Gentile, or maybe even Democrat and Republican! Through his Spirit he calls us and enables us to be who we are and are becoming in him, so that we may live in union with Christ by his Spirit in gratitude to God our Father. And we need to do that in our daily lives, personal, social, and political. Christ has assumed and redeemed our humanity, and he graciously grants us the freedom and opportunity and responsibility to be his brothers and sisters in society. That's my paradigm, for what it's worth.

Appendix B

God, Woody Allen, and Job

"I am the loyal opposition," Woody Allen once remarked to express his ambivalence towards God. Allen's disturbing humor about God and evil, faith and doubt, and love and death warrants the attention of anyone who wonders about God. "If it turns out that there is a God," Boris (Woody Allen) concludes in *Love and Death*, "I don't think that he's evil. I think that the worst you can say about him is that basically he is an underachiever." "Even if he exists," Bob (Alan Alda) declares in *Everyone Says I Love You*, "he's done such a terrible job, it's a wonder why people don't get together and file a class action suit against him."

Appreciating his theological comedy while questioning his apparent conclusions, I feel a similar sense of "loyal opposition" to Woody Allen. I will first examine several of Allen's most theological essays and films that represent his grounds for questioning whether God exists, focusing on the relation of faith and doubt, as well as on God and evil. Although caricature is part and parcel of the comedic filmmaker's craft, Allen addresses serious issues with implicit worldview assumptions that this essay will unearth. (I assume that consistent theological ideas which recur throughout his life's work reflect his worldview, given, of course, that the genre of comedy differs from prose.) I will then discuss the Joban and crucified Jesus' questioning of God as a *more* radical alternative to Allen's protest. While Job and Jesus were both deeply anguished by the ostensible absence of God, their faith embraced doubt and did not resolve the mystery of evil. These ancient biblical protests comprised greater ambiguity than the modern filmmaker Woody Allen, who tends to resolve the ambiguity in favor of doubt, although I suspect God himself smiles at his theological comedy.

Fully Human

The Search for Certainty

"I am plagued by doubts," Allen admits. "What if everything is an illusion and nothing exists? In that case, I definitely overpaid for my carpet."[1] In an essay entitled "Mr. Big," Allen depicts a woman who needs to know with "absolute certainty" that God exists and so hires a private detective to find God. "That's right," she says, "God. The Creator, the Underlying Principle, the First Cause of Things, the All Encompassing. I want you to find Him for me." The detective then begins to search for "Mr. Big."[2]

"Of course there's a you-know-what," asserts his first lead, Rabbi Itzhak Wiseman, "but I'm not even allowed to say His name or He'll strike me dead, which I could never understand why someone is so touchy about having his name said." After listening to the Rabbi's appeal to the omnipotent God of the Bible who delivered the Israelites out of bondage and chose them as His people — in exchange for a large payoff ("the old protection racket," he notes) — the detective next interviews gangster and avowed atheist Chicago Phil. "There's no Mr. Big," he insists. "I couldn't pass all those bad checks or screw society the way I do if for one second I was able to recognize any authentic sense of Being. The universe is strictly phenomenological. Nothing's eternal. It's all meaningless."[3]

The private eye tries to add it all up at a local pub, but it makes no sense: "Socrates was a suicide — or so they said. Christ was murdered. Nietzsche went nuts. If there was someone out there, He sure as hell didn't want anybody to know it." He poses the possibility to his client that Kierkegaard might have been right, namely, that "you can never really *know*. Only have faith. . . . Don't be so rational." Sergeant Reed of Homicide interrupts their discussion: "You still looking for God . . . An all-powerful Being? Great Oneness, Creator of the Universe? First Cause of All Things?" "That's right," the private eye replies. "Somebody with that description just showed up at the morgue. You better get down here right away," advises the sergeant. "It's the work of an existentialist. We're sure of that. . . . Haphazard way how it was done. Doesn't seem to be any system followed. Impulse." The detective concludes that life is now absurd and so ends the woman's quest for "absolute certainty."[4]

---

1 *Without Feathers* (NY: Random House, 1975), 6.
2 *Getting Even* (NY: Random House, 1971), 139ff.
3 Ibid., 141ff.
4 Ibid., 144ff.

Appendix B

Nearly twenty years later, one of Allen's most mature films, *Hannah and Her Sisters*, portrays the same relation of certainty and absurdity. Mickey (Woody Allen) searches for the meaning of life amidst his hypochondriacal fear of sickness and death with an equally neurotic cast of characters: Hannah (Mia Farrow), formerly married to Mickey and now married to Elliot (Michael Caine), who falls in love with one of Hannah's sisters, Lee (Barbara Hershey), who lives with a misanthropic artist, Frederick (Max von Sydow). Holly (Dianne Wiest) is Hannah's other sister, who medicates her constant anxieties and insecurities with cocaine.

Mickey, anguished by the uncertainty and unpredictability of life and terrified by the only certainty of life — the inevitability of death — quits his job as a television comedy writer. He embarks upon a religious quest to avert the ruinous conclusion that nothing matters, since "The only absolute knowledge attainable by man is that life is meaningless" (a quotation by Tolstoy that the filmmaker inserts into his film). The beauty and certainty of Catholicism initially attract him until a priest counsels a blind leap of faith in lieu of proof. Mickey then tells a Hare Krishna adherent that he meets on the street that he abandoned his Jewish upbringing and his momentary attraction to Catholicism and its belief, "die now, pay later." He confesses an attraction to belief in reincarnation but becomes too anxious about where his soul will actually go — over to another human or to a moose or an aardvark? He also dismisses Nietzsche's theory of eternal recurrence when he muses, "Great. That means I'll have to sit through the Ice Capades again."

His depression deepens. Faced with the prospect of a godless universe, he aims a rifle toward his head but suddenly wonders, "What if I'm wrong?" Again he insists on the either/or option: certainty or nothing. "In a godless universe," he concedes, "I don't want to go on living." While perspiring and debating with himself, he accidentally triggers the rifle, although the bullet misses him and shatters a mirror. He leaves his room to ruminate while he wanders the streets so that he can put life back into rational perspective. He meanders into a movie theater that is showing *Duck Soup*, a Marx Brothers' movie that helps him come to terms with the absurdity of life. Considering the worst prospect in life — "there's no God, and you only go around once" — he concludes to enjoy life while it lasts and not to seek answers to unanswerable questions. He also considers the best outcome — maybe, just maybe, there is a God and an afterlife — although he reaffirms that no one can know for sure. Comedy thus enables Mickey to sustain the absurdity of life's struggles.⁵

Although love had disappointed him in his first marriage, the Marx Brothers' comedic absurdity has now readied him to love again. In the final scene, while reflecting on the resiliency of the human heart, Mickey hugs Holly, now his second wife; she in turn informs him that she is pregnant. This commitment to a new wife and their progeny quells his crisis and ends his search.⁶ In Kierkegaardian categories, he has entered the ethical but not the religious sphere. Allen commends laughter and love — represented by the Marx Brothers' movie and marriage and pregnancy, respectively — but not faith to accept the absurdity of life. Even in a godless universe, one can create meaning in life. Allen opts for Camus — tempered by Groucho Marx! — over Kierkegaard.

The lack of faith's certainty plagues Mickey and prevents a leap of faith, given that Allen bases Mickey's quest on the false dilemma of certainty or absurdity. Worldview assumptions like faith commitments might not make good material for comedy, but Allen's implicit assumptions about the epistemic status of theological affirmations do guide how Mickey frames and resolves his crisis. The quest for absolute certainty leads him to embrace absurdity as the reasonable alternative certainty. Allen appears to opt out of ambiguity — faith living with, even embracing, doubt — in favor of absurdity — laughing at the meaningless of life.

In addition to the uncertainty of faith, Allen also introduces another classic objection to faith in Hannah: "If there's a God," Mickey queries his parent, "why is ethere so much evil in the world? . . . Why were there Nazis?" "How the hell do I know why there were Nazis?" his father retorts. "I don't even know how the can opener works."⁷ The problem of evil serves as a second key ground for doubt implicit in Allen's work.

---

5 Allen substitutes the myth of Freedonia (Duck Soup) in place of the myth of Sisyphus. Also cf. the chorus of ghosts in Allen's *Everyone Says I Love You* singing at a funeral: "Enjoy yourself, enjoy yourself, it's later than you think."

6 Cf. Allen's self-criticism that this film was too neat, tidy, and happy in the end, and that he lacked the nerve to recapitulate the Tolstoy quotation on the meaningless of life (*Woody Allen on Woody Allen: In Conversation with Stig Bjorkman* [NY: Grove Press, 1993], 156). Also cf. Allen's ironic point in *The Purple Rose of Cairo* when Cecilia (Mia Farrow) declares, God is "a reason for everything. Otherwise, it'd be like a movie without a point and no happy ending." Cecelia's own personal story does not have a happy ending, but movie-going sustains her through her hardships.

7 Cf. Allen's essay, "My Speech to the Graduates," on the limits of science, as well as religion, for "modern man" — that is, "any person born after Nietzsche's edict that

Appendix B

The Problem of Evil

"Man does not bring on his own unhappiness," Allen declares, "and suffering is really God's will, although why He gets such a kick out of it is beyond me."[8] *Crimes and Misdemeanors*, Allen's most explicitly theological, and one of his best films, probes life in a world without God and responds to Dostoevsky's dictum: "If God does not exist, then all things are permitted." He uses that dictum to pose the question: "Do the eyes of God see all?"

Judah Rosenthal (Marlin Landau) is an ophthalmologist who, despite his ability to correct others' vision, ironically lacks moral vision. He has an affair with Dolores Paley (Angelica Huston). As their "fatal attraction" grows, Jack (Jerry Orbach) counsels his brother that a hitman can take care of this "problem" (i.e., Dolores). Judah sums up his brother's view of life — "Jack lives in the real world" — and after a momentary wrestling with the morality of murder, he hires the hitman to do the deed.

Ben (Sam Waterston) is a rabbi who, despite his excellent moral vision, ironically is going blind. In a state of delirium, Judah believes that Ben counsels him to confess his wrongdoing, for the world has a "moral structure" based on a "higher power." Ben believes that God sees what Judah has done. Judah replies to Ben, "You live in the Kingdom of Heaven."[9]

In a flashback of his childhood, Judah recalls his father Sol's (David S. Howard) pronouncement at the dinner table: "The eyes of God see all." Similar to the Solomon of Proverbs, this Sol announces that the righteous shall be rewarded and the wicked punished. "If he's caught," retorts Aunt May (Anna Berger). Because she considers evil as evidence that the world lacks a moral structure, she challenges Sol to choose between God and truth. Shall Sol either believe in God or see the world's injustices? Without hesitation, Sol chooses God over the truth of reality.

'God is dead,' but before the hit recording 'I Wanna Hold Your Hand.'" Commenting on a toaster that has not worked properly for years, he ponders, "Are we counting on nuts and bolts and electricity to solve our problems?" "And where is science when one ponders the eternal riddles?" *Side Effects* (NY: Random House, 1981), 58ff.

8 *Getting Even*, 68.

9 Cf. Allen's comment that Ben "has genuine faith ... But as the author, *I* think that Ben is blind even before he's blind, because he doesn't see what's real in the world. But he's lucky, cause he has his naiveté ... One can argue that he understands (the reality of life) more deeply than the others. I don't think so myself. I think he understands it less, and that's why I wanted to make him blind. I feel that his faith is blind. It will work, but it requires closing your eyes to reality" (*Woody Allen on Woody Allen*, 223; emphasis Allen's).

Meanwhile, Clifford Stern (Woody Allen) — who describes himself as having "great depth and smoldering sensuality" — films documentaries on topics such as leukemia and toxic waste. His current documentary interviews Prof. Louis Levy (Martin Bergmann), who is gripped by life's paradoxes. In the shadow of the Holocaust, the professor ponders why a so-called just and moral God would command Abraham to sacrifice his son Isaac. In light of life's injustices, he cannot find comfort in Ben and Sol's God, who supposedly governs the world justly, or in Jack and Aunt May's "realistic" view — that "might makes right." Prof. Levy sees but eventually cannot tolerate the ambiguities of life. His suicide note simply reads, "I've gone out the window."

Crimes and Misdemeanors' multiple characters portray ironic contrasts to reject the traditional doctrine of retribution (that is, you reap what you sow). The rabbi goes blind while the ophthalmologist gets off scot-free; in fact, he not only evades punishment (from God, the state, or even his own conscience), but he also prospers and lives happily ever after, walking off with his wife in the end while feeling no compunction for his crime.

Allen's film, however, does not counsel despair. It suggests that individuals assume responsibility for their actions; otherwise, moral chaos will ensue. Allen follows Camus to respond to Doestoevsky: in a world without God, the implicit theology of this film intimates that individuals themselves must practice moral responsibility "In the absence of a god or something," as Cliff says to Judah, a murderer "is forced to face that responsibility himself" — a notion that Judah dismisses as "fiction." But a documentary clip of Prof. Levy contains the last word and speaks for Allen: "We define ourselves by the choices we have made. We are, in fact, the sum total of our choices. . . . It is only we, with our capacity to love, that gives meaning to the indifferent universe." Allen strikes, once again, the Camusian chords: there is no intrinsic meaning to human existence, so humans should defiantly — or humorously, for Allen — create their own meaning in a purposeless world.

Likewise, in an essay entitled "The Condemned," Allen portrays the character Cloquet, who "hated reality but realized it was still the only place to get a good steak."[10] In this story, Cloquet contemplates whether to shoot the infamous Fascist informer Brisseau. While clutching his pistol, he considers the moral ramifications of his contemplated deed: "By choosing my action, I choose it for all mankind. But what if everyone in the world

---

10 *Side Effects*, 9ff.

behaved like me and came here and shot Brisseau through the ear. What a mess!" So he drops the revolver and flees.[11]

Brisseau is nevertheless murdered, and Cloquet is arrested as a suspect. While in jail, he reflects on whether or not there is still time to convert from atheism but decides to "meet my fate alone. There is no God. There is no purpose to life. Nothing lasts.... Why go through this hollow charade called life? Why, except that somewhere within us a voice says, 'Live.' Always, from some inner region, we hear the command, 'Keep living.' Cloquet recognizes the voice; it was his insurance salesman. *Naturally*, he thought — *Fishbein doesn't want to pay off.*" While he excogitates these questions, the jailer notifies him that the real murderer has confessed. He is now free to go, and the thought of freedom "simultaneously exhilarated and terrified" him.[12]

Allen's play *God* similarly suggests the necessity of exercising human freedom in a world without God. In this play, Hepatitis, a writer of a play entitled "The Slave," discusses the ending of the play with the lead actor named Diabetes. While they debate the final scene, another character, Trichinosis, proposes that they call on Zeus (a *Deus ex machina*) to descend dramatically from on high to save the humble hopeless slave Diabetes. "But if God saves everything," the writer objects, "man is not responsible for his actions." "You wonder why you're not invited to more parties," the actor quips. "I don't accept it," the writer persists. "I'm a free man and don't need God flying in to save my play. I'm a good writer." But an impressive demonstration of the God machine and a reasonable rental rate convince the writer to use it.[13]

Hepatitis' play begins with Diabetes' declaration, "I don't want to be free. I like it this way. I know what's expected of me. I'm taken care of. I don't have to make any choices. I was born a slave and I'll die a slave. I have no anxiety." "Freedom is dangerous," continues Diabetes the slave. "If there's a war, who do you think gets killed? The free people. But we're safe because no matter who's in power, they all need someone to do the heavy cleaning."[14]

---

11 Boris (Woody Allen) considers murder in *Love and Death* and asks, "What if everybody acted like this? It'd be a world full of murderers. Do you know what that would do to property values?"

12 *Side Effects*, 15ff.

13 *Without Feathers*, 125ff., 143ff., 150ff.

14 Ibid., 154ff.

The king enters and asks Diabetes one and only question, "Is there a god?" When Diabetes says "Yes," the king replies, "If there is a god, then man is not responsible and I will surely be judged for my sins. . . . This is the worst possible news." As the king prepares to behead the slave, Diabetes calls upon Zeus, but the God machine gets stuck and the lowering wire strangles him. A messenger reads a telegram, "God is dead. Stop. You're on your own."[15]

The Biblical Protest

Allen's protest that humans must confront the absurdity of life on their own presents an ironic contrast with Job, the biblical poet of protest, who also questions whether God justly governs the universe. While he does not question God's existence or power, he does experience the problem of God's justice with greater ambiguity than even the modern filmmaker Allen.

Job, whom God himself described as "blameless and upright" (Job 1:8), suffers without measure. Although his friends initially come to comfort him — wisely sitting in silence with him, not daring to utter a word — they soon reduce the complexity of his experience to a single formula: Repent of your sins! Assuming the traditional proverbial wisdom discussed throughout the book of Proverbs — the righteous are rewarded and sinners suffer — they infer that the suffering Job must submit to God's correction to receive his forgiveness. "Who, being innocent, has ever perished?" (4:7a) queried one of the friends. *If* you repent, they judge, then God will forgive you. In a wonderful twist of irony, God finally commands them, not Job, to repent of their presumptuous folly, and he accepts Job's prayer and intercession for them (42:8).[16]

The book of Job challenges a simplistic understanding of the traditional doctrine of retribution that prevails throughout Proverbs. (Solomon himself is wise enough to recognize exceptions to this rule of life — unlike Sol, who accepted Aunt May's false dilemma that one must choose between God and truth.) Job's friends err in proclaiming "timeless truth," rather

---

15 Ibid., 170ff. Also cf. The Greek chorus in *Mighty Aphrodite*, which calls Zeus — "most potent of gods!" — for help but only gets his answering machine.

16 *Annie Hall* contains a scene where a pretentious university professor is pontificating on Marshall McLuhan's theory of media. Alvy Singer (Woody Allen) gets so fed up that he suddenly pulls out McLuhan himself from behind a post, and McLuhan humbles the boorish pseudo-intellectual: "You know nothing of my work!" Allen then turns to the camera and says, "If only life were like this!"

Appendix B

than addressing their friend in his concrete situation. Displaying a lack of wisdom in their attempt to apply wisdom, they rely on religious cliches. When fools indiscriminately apply Solomon's doctrine, they both distort wisdom and dehumanize people in need.

While Job does begin as the submissive, saintly sufferer who refuses to question God (chaps. 1 & 2), sharing the traditional theology of his friends and even rejoicing in his calamity (1:21), he soon complains with a bitter cry (chap. 3ff.): Why was I born? How long can I tolerate these miserable comforters? What have I done to deserve God's chastisement? Where is God that I may accuse him? How may I contend with God himself? Who will take up my cause and intercede on my behalf?

Job experiences an unbearable tension: the presence and absence of God. Job *knows* whom he *accuses*. He sees the ambiguities of life with more depth and torment than his friends, who are quick to resolve the ambiguity. Unlike them — and perhaps Allen as well — he now lives with both faith and doubt.

Challenging the limits of human wisdom and asserting the majesty of divine transcendence (chap. 38ff.), God does question Job's presumption to know how God does and should govern the universe. Even though God asked his own questions of Job, he never rebuked Job's cry of complaint; in fact, he permitted Job's lengthy speeches and vindicated Job over and against the presumptuous theology of his friends.[17]

The book of Job suggests two insights regarding the problem of human suffering. First, humans must acknowledge the limits of their wisdom. Since Adam, humans have presumed to know good and evil (Gen. 3:5), attempting to extend what they know about the mystery and complexity of life. The Greeks learned in order to comprehend, as Abraham Joshua Heschel has said; the Hebrews learned in order to revere.[18] Job finally confesses, "Surely I spoke of things I did not understand, things too

---

17 Cp. Allen's essay, "The Scrolls" — "translated fragments" of Job and other biblical passages (though their authenticity is in doubt since the word "Oldsmobile" appears in the texts). When Job complained to God that he was better off without God, in Allen's re-creation, God only questioned but never commended the questioner Job. Also cp. Allen's rendition of the Abraham and Isaac story, in which Abraham declares, "The faithful do not question," as he prepares to sacrifice his son Isaac until God interrupts him to tell him, "I was only joking!" (ibid., 22ff.).

18 My paraphrase is a recurrent theme of of Heschel's. See his *God in Search of Man: A Philosophy of Judaism* (NY: Farrar, Straus and Girous, 1955) and *The Prophets* Vols. 1 & 2 (NY: Harper, 1962).

wonderful for me to know" (42:3). Christians and moderns have much to learn from the Hebraic mind, including an epistemology that presupposes humility. "God is silent," Allen remarks; "now if we can only get Man to shut up."[19]

Secondly, God himself speaks to Job. Even though he confronts Job's presumption, proclaiming to Job the grandeur of creation, he finally commends Job and condemns the folly of his friends' counsel. God speaks, humbling yet comforting Job by his appearance. Unlike a *Deus ex machina* — a god who is extraordinarily present but ordinarily absent — Job apprehends that God is his God. Beyond any intellectual resolution to the problem of unmerited human suffering, Job repents of the human propensity to control God with one's questions or answers and simply acknowledges, "My ears had heard of you, but now my eyes have seen you" (42:5).

Job perceives that he can see God on the underside of life. Sol's simplistic slogan — God over truth — forces the sufferer to choose between God and the reality of one's own experience, a choice that Aunt May reasonably argues would favor experience in light of life's tragedies. Job — unlike Prof. Levy, who perceives but cannot tolerate ambiguity — brings his questions and complaints to God. Job heightens the tensions of *Crimes and Misdemeanors*. The biblical poet and man of exemplary faith questions God himself, who in turn challenges but then commends the one who dares to confront the Almighty, and thereby *enlarges* the categories of experience: Job can now live with both faith and doubt, because God is his advocate. While Allen agonizes over ambiguity, Job embraces both faith and doubt; he continues to believe because of, not despite, his protest. He knows whom he accuses.

Jesus on the cross poses the problem with unmitigated intensity: "My God, my God, why have you forsaken me?"[20] Did God close his eyes? Did Jesus' cry indicate that God is so holy and transcendent that he could not bear to look upon those who sin or suffer? If so, the salvation of the world and the comfort of those who despair hinge upon a tragic human figure abandoned by his own Father. Or does Jesus' cry of God-forsakenness underscore God's identification and solidarity with people, especially in their need? The psalmist David, in the tradition of Job, originally uses

---

19 *Side Effects*, 5.

20 Or in Allen's version, "My Lord, my Lord! What has Thou done, lately?" *Without Feathers*, 25.

Appendix B

these very words to complain to God (Ps. 22) — yet David also praises God as his and Israel's deliverer in the second half of this psalm, just as Job eventually perceives God as his defender. God himself takes up David's cry, Job's cry, our cry of complaint. From his birth unto death, Christ stood where we stand and offered up his representative humanity as an oblation to God his Father on our behalf. From Gethsemane to Golgotha, God intensified his presence with and for sinners, outcasts, and those who suffer without relief. Hence, while Allen's caricature of God humorously and rightly dismisses a "god of the gaps," Jesus' incarnational solidarity with us reveals the heart and presence of God the Father for suffering humanity.

The Pharisees of Jesus' day cannot relate to outcasts and sinners. Like Job's friends, they distort truth and dehumanize people. Jesus scandalizes these self-righteous saints by preferring to eat and drink — that is, to have fellowship — with outcasts and sinners. Jesus' truth is for humanity! He does not accept Aunt May's false dilemma between God and truth. He intervenes in the lives of the broken-hearted and speaks God's truth on behalf of those in need, so that they might apprehend God in the midst of their agony and despair.

The Gospel presupposes God's forgiving grace and sustaining presence for sinners, outcasts, and those marginalized by the vicissitudes of life. Jesus protects the woman caught in adultery from the stones of self-righteous "saints," for he stands as her advocate before telling her to sin no longer. The prodigal son only serves as a paradigm of repentance because the forgiving father goes out to the son to embrace him and to ground his repentance in the father's gracious and joyous love for his son. "But while he was still along way off, his father saw him" (Luke 15:20): yes, the eyes of God are on the world, but not merely to see all. For the person in need, God is somewhere rather than everywhere.[21] To use the

---

21 In an essay, "Notes from the Overfed (After reading Dostoevsky and the new 'Weight Watchers' magazine on the same plane trip)," Allen creates a dialogue (and another false dilemma) between an overweight nephew who questions God and his uncle who can only affirm the abstraction that "God is everywhere." "I do not believe in God," the nephew declares. "Could it not be simply that we are alone and aimless," he continues, "doomed to wander in an indifferent universe, with no hope of salvation, nor any prospect except misery, death, and the empty reality of nothing?" "You wonder why you're not invited to more parties!" his uncle retorts. "Good nephew," he insists, "there is a God, despite what you think, and He is everywhere. Yes! Everywhere!" "If God is everywhere," the nephew replies, "then He is in food .... Don't you see? Fat is everything! Unless, of course, you're overweight" (*Getting Even*, 84ff.).

metaphor of *Crimes and Misdemeanors*, God sees the agony and distress of those in need *and bears* their sorrows on his divine heart, displayed in the life and ministry of Jesus.

In Woody Allen's *Manhattan*, Isaac (Woody Allen) looks Tracy (Mariel Hemingway) in the eye and observes, "You're God's answer to Job." The Gospel, however, points beyond human love to the humanity of Christ, who embodies God's love for the needy and who sees life from the humiliation of his cross. Those who suffer may cry with the one who cries out in their place and on their behalf "My God, my God, why have you forsaken me?" — and apprehend and acknowledge God's advocacy for them.

Conclusion

Woody Allen, to summarize my critique, consistently employs false dilemmas — for example, faith or doubt, God or truth — not only because he writes comedy, but also because his implicit worldview assumptions govern how he portrays and addresses belief in God. He humorously and helpfully explores the uncertainty of faith in an all-loving and all-powerful God in light of the ambiguities of life, but he ultimately and ironically tends to resolve the ambiguity of faith living with doubt in favor of doubt alone. Job and Jesus, on the other hand, sustain the ambiguity of faith living with doubt by addressing prayers of protest to God himself and thus, if anything, *increase* the tension perceived by Allen. Faith chastened by doubt and evil, therefore, permits those who question God to cry out to the Son in his passion and agony on behalf of suffering humanity.

Allen does render Christian scholars a service, however, by forging his theology — which is to say, his musings and doubts about God's existence — in the public medium of film. As God's "loyal opposition," he cannot seem to ignore God. And he provokes Christians to consider both with gravity and with levity absurd aspects of their faith in God, such as the uncertainty of faith and the problem of evil. Even those who question Allen's implicit theology can still benefit from his unique way of doing theology, especially as they serve the God of the world and the God who laughs.

www.ingramcontent.com/pod-product-compliance
Lightning Source LLC
Chambersburg PA
CBHW051938160426
43198CB00013B/2209